STEP AHEAD C

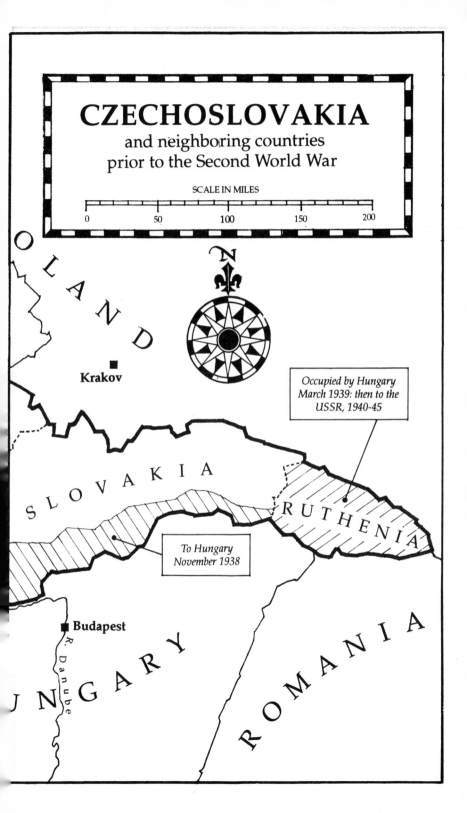

CZECHOSLOVAKIA
and neighboring countries
prior to the Second World War

SCALE IN MILES

0   50   100   150   200

N

POLAND

Krakov

Occupied by Hungary
March 1939: then to the
USSR, 1940-45

SLOVAKIA

RUTHENIA

To Hungary
November 1938

Budapest

R. Danube

HUNGARY

ROMANIA

STEP
AHEAD
OF
DISASTER

EUGENE von TEUBER
WITH
BASIL ENTWISTLE

GROSVENOR

First published 1993 by
GROSVENOR USA
3735 Cherry Avenue NE
Salem, Oregon 97303

Also available from Grosvenor Books at:

54 Lyford Road
London SW18 3JJ
UK

226 Kooyong Road
Toorak, VIC 3142
Australia

Suite 405, 251 Bank Street
Ottawa, Ontario K2P 1X3
Canada

PO Box 1834
Wellington
New Zealand

Library of Congress Cataloging-in-Publication Data

Von Teuber, Eugene
  Step ahead of disaster / Eugene von Teuber with Basil Entwistle:
foreword by Michael Novak.
       p.   cm.
  ISBN 1-85239-510-9
  1. Von Teuber, Eugene. 2. World War, 1939-1945 – Personal
narratives, Czech. 3. Nobility – Czech Republic – Biography.
4. World War, 1939-1945 – Czechoslovakia. 5. Czechoslovakia –
History – 1939-1945. I. Entwistle, Basil. II. Title.
D811.5.V65   1993
940.54'82437 – dc20   93-8257
                                                                    CIP

Book design: Blair Cummock
Cover design: W Cameron Johnson

Typeset in Palatino by Paragon Typesetters, Chester, England
Printed by Biddles of Guildford, England

Contents

Foreword
by Michael Novak

A CRACKING good story is not often simply told as honest autobiography. In this extraordinary autobiography, the reader will learn much vivid detail about the horrors of the twentieth century, from a point of view that would normally have escaped him: that of the eldest son of a wealthy aristocratic family of Imperial Austria, the dispossessed heir to a distinguished estate in the deer-filled hills and lake country of Moravia. Through Eugene von Teuber and his contacts, the reader will meet Adolph Hitler, Tomáš Masaryk (on his sickbed), and stand in the palace window from which, as the story unfolds, Jan Masaryk will be thrown to his death. And the reader will experience from street and village level what the arrival of Communism in 1948 meant to daily life.

Within the pages of this brief book, the world of the twentieth century turns upside down. A noble family of proud aristocrats is humbled, imprisoned, reduced to slave labor, and their once great and manicured properties are pushed into ruin.

In addition, turning the pages rapidly as suspense mounts, the reader will follow the efforts of the young aristocrat, married to a young Californian of striking beauty, to rescue their children (from the Nazis) and later his parents (from the Communists). The underlying story, however, is one of conversion – a conversion first to fearless personal honesty, then to the humble charity of the gospels.

It will sound like exaggeration, but it is true. This book includes adventure, a tale of personal transformation, a portrait of the fragile beauty of the feudal order and its sudden shattering under the clatter of goose-stepping soldiers. One is witness to cultural animosities and frictions among the Austrians, Germans, Czechs and Slovaks and, above all, the omnipresent feeling and weight of European class-consciousness — whose bitter fruit is the rise of the mindless egalitarianism of the ''people's courts.''

Yet at the heart of the story lies the influence of the Oxford Group, the friends of Frank Buchman, upon the life of Eugene von Teuber, who had left his father's home to prepare himself for his inheritance by acquiring an international education. The first part of this conversion happens off-stage, before this narrative actually begins. But in reminiscence at one point Eugene does recall how Buchman and his friends taught him, for the first time, to take seriously in deeds what he had long believed. Until then, he says, he had carried his beliefs lightly — they barely, if at all, altered his way of living, which was then ruled by routines, customs and conventional viewpoints. Cautiously, Eugene began to let conscience bite behavior. Slowly, his life began to change, prudently, wisely, but inexorably.

After a stay in Britain, von Teuber went to America, because he wished to drink deeply the ideal of classlessness and universal opportunity that the United States stood for. His father's approval for this stay in America was conditioned on Eugene's not marrying an American woman. But a Californian — spirited and capable of depths like his, proved too much for his resolution; and the young woman, Dorothy, set herself to mastering the subtle arts that would be expected of a spouse of the high station she would assume in Czechoslovakia. She passed her first test, over a dinner in San Francisco with a formal and stuffy emissary of the family, not without some humorous incidents, and the marriage went forward with tentative parental consent. In the feudal order, little was as important as family.

The narrative begins with Eugene and Dorothy on their first visit to the family estate; when at the first formal dinner the elegant Dorothy, dancing gracefully in her green chiffon dress, conquers family anxieties with flying colors, one is reminded, just a little, of Eliza Doolittle in *My Fair Lady*. The narrative moves a little slower through these early pages of reminiscence and domesticity, but every detail becomes important in later stages of the tale. For Eugene introduces personalities – the family chauffeur, for example – who later came to hold the family fate in their hands. With brutal but forgiving frankness, Eugene records in crucial detail the pride and prejudice in daily intercouse that had characterized Central Europe for hundreds of years.

I found these details absolutely compelling, for my own great-grandfather in Slovakia was a forester on the estate of a Hungarian noble family. (In a parallel irony of history, my younger brother, as an instructor at the University of Notre Dame, has as one of his students the dispossessed son of that same family.) It goes without saying that the role of the Moravian foresters on the days of the great hunts, described with loving detail and universal sympathy by Eugene von Teuber, was to me of intense interest. It is true that sharing the one Catholic faith was a bond among classes and nationalities in the Austro-Hungarian Empire; but it is also true that the fixity of station and role, together with inevitable unfairness and small cruelties, lodged in family memory even when there was no special reason for bitterness. It was greatly to Eugene von Teuber's credit that he himself came to perceive this and, in Buchman's spirit, decided to act upon this perception, even to the loss of his inheritance. The night on which this break with his father occurred is a night of great drama, an axis on which this book turns.

One admires the many moments of intense drama in this book, but even more the exquisite eye for detail and economy of expression exercised by its disciplined author – and, one must add, by his wife, who herself tells the tale of how she went behind German lines, without her husband, to bring her two young children to safety, after the perfidious lightning-like occupation of Czechoslovakia by Adolph Hitler's exultant armies. In finding ways through impassable obstacles, Dorothy's quick wit and cold courage were every inch a match for her husband's.

Simple as this book is, then, and in a sense naively told, without artifice or false dramatization, its story is one of the classics of our era. Few books so well convey the feeling of a thousand-year era collapsing, or reveal the character of an aristocratic heir to privilege whose vision throughout remains moral and truthful, unbounded by considerations solely of class or custom.

I think I shall never forget the image of Eugene's father, the great Count, and his once prideful mother, both in their eighties, forbidden to walk on the sidewalks, forced to wear the white armbands that marked collaborators with the Germans, being spat upon and sometimes struck, and serving the Communist state as menial servants, the one shuffling along carrying bricks, the other scrubbing the floors of public buildings. Or forget the image of their wrecked and empty palace, its red sofa slashed by multiple bayonet and knife strokes. On the wall still hangs, askew, the dominating portrait of the Countess and four-year-old Eugene – her eyes have been shot out by bullets fired at close range.

Yet to me, perhaps, the most moving passages are those in which Eugene quite unflatteringly depicts his parents as they were before their fall, love them as he did, and then those which record matter-of-factly the transformation in their spirits under the most awful social convulsions. The von Teubers proved themselves to have been a noble family indeed, in ways to which mere birth alone cannot give title.

It is sad, perhaps, that this book was not published years ago. Yet there is something providential in its appearance after the "velvet revolution" of 1989, after the fall of Communism, and after the emergence of a free society closer to Eugene von Teuber's dreams – dreams he learned from Masaryk, from his sojourn in the United States, and from the Oxford Group. For the book has no polemical or partisan edge, but stands, rather, as a touching record of events that happened while our generations lived on this earth. It conveys masterfully certain details of daily life that must not be forgotten. It inspires us to live with greater seriousness, not to be so easily lulled or fooled, and to remember the few basic things: truth, conscience, sympathy, humble charity. These suffice.

Washington, D.C.
May 20, 1993

Introduction

CZECHOSLOVAKIA was for Americans perhaps the most intriguing of the six nations of Eastern Europe whose transformation shook the world during the last six months of 1989. Its revolution was the smoothest, spanning only seven weeks and without the loss of a single life. Czechoslovakia was also the most perplexing of countries, artificially created out of the Austro-Hungarian empire, and comprising Czechs, Slovaks, Hungarians, Austrians, Germans and other minorities.

Its founding father, Tomáš Masaryk, set out to build a democratic union modeled on the Swiss Federation and the United States. Yet the proud and divergent cultures contained within its borders are still at odds today. Moreover, during its short history, the country has undergone four traumatic changes, from independence to Nazi occupation, to Soviet satellite, to regained independence, and now most recently to the division of the country into two separate nations, Czech and Slovak. As we Americans listened to President Vaclác Havel addressing Congress many of us were heartened as well as challenged by his wisdom and humility. What manner of people, we wondered, are these Czechs?

Shortly after the nation regained its independence a manuscript came into my hands, written by a friend, Eugene von Teuber, which threw light on the stuff of which the nation was made – its longings, sufferings, strengths and weaknesses. As a teenager Teuber had witnessed the country's birth when the government distributed part of his father's large estates among tenant farmers; as a young man

1

preparing himself to administer the property, he lived through the mounting tensions between Czechs and German-Austrians which involved his aristocratic family and their hundreds of workers; then, when Hitler's troops were quartered on the estate, he and his wife and children escaped by a hair's breadth the German military tidal wave at the start of World War II.

Even more traumatic were Gene Teuber's adventures at war's end when he set out to rescue his parents and brother, who had been dragged by the Communists from their 99-room castle to concentration camp and prison on the eve of Stalinist oppression.

Gene Teuber died with his manuscript still in rough form. I had known him for thirty years and appreciated his mind-set, his aspirations and his vivid personality. When his sons asked me to put their father's writing into shape for publication I gladly responded. I found a detailed account, which required no additions, merely a streamlining of his dramatic story.

Here are the absorbing adventures of a Czech-Austrian-American, barely running ahead of disaster. Here also is the moving tale of a man breaking free from a web of inherited prejudices and risking life and liberty to save those dear to him. As we Americans try to grasp the significance of events unfolding among the peoples of Eastern Europe, we can identify with the common humanity of those pictured in this vivid chronicle.

Basil Entwistle

1

Homecoming

THE STEWARD knocked on our cabin door. "We're here, sir!"

Six o'clock. I glanced at the salt-laden mist seeping in through the open porthole and reached over to shake my wife gently. "Darling, we're coming in."

The blue eyes opened wide and in a moment she was up. A few minutes later I was following her slim brown legs as she leapt up the ship's broad stairs, hair streaming behind her, to the wet, slippery deck and the tingling blast of a cold early summer dawn in the old Hanseatic port of Bremen. The prow of *Europa* was nudging its way into the harbor, then scraping against the slimy, barnacled piles of the dock, launching the grey-white sea-gulls from their sedate perches, screeching indignantly.

We watched brawny bared arms of seamen uncoiling heavy hemp ropes, tossing them expertly to strong hands below. Soon the decks were full of clattering passengers with sloppily bound wicker baskets, their children clutching ample skirts, and chic suited men and women stepping distastefully aside from the crowd.

For Dorothy, my young American wife of three years, this was her first glimpse of the "Old World." It was also the first step on my visit home to present her to my Austrian parents living on our estates in Czechoslovakia. When my autocratic father agreed to my extended visit to the United States, his one stipulation had been, "Gene, do whatever you want over there – except marry an American girl." As I watched over her now, surveying the scene, I wondered how this naive, enthusiastic, freedom-loving young American would react to the age-old customs and traditions of our people. And how, I wondered, would my conservative family react to her!

My attention was distracted as the gang plank clanked down on the pier and through the grey haze a horde of small urchins clambered up to reach the passengers with newspapers. One of them raucously shouted the headlines: "Hitler Consolidates Power in Germany," as he thrust papers at me with one hand, holding out his other small paw for the price plus tip. I reached for *Die Frankfurter, The Times* of London, *Zürcher Zeitung*. All used Hitler's term *Gleichschaltung*, coordination, to describe his action. "Malicious double-talk," I muttered.

The year was 1933. Each morning on the voyage the ship's newspaper had been slipped under our door, but the news from Europe was brief, and probably phrased to instill a sense of calm among the passengers as they lounged under the fitful sunshine. One morning our German ship's captain had perched casually on the end of my deck chair and I remarked, "This Hitler seems a queer one to be able to gain as much support as the cables imply."

He waved away my doubts into the ocean haze: "Oh, Germans must always have someone to follow. You Austrians must know that! Give Hitler credit for cleaning up Berlin." Berlin had a reputation as the most immoral city in Europe. The captain's eyes lit up. "And the youth – they love their uniforms, their songs and their Führer. Yes, good clean boys and girls. We shall all be glad for what he's doing." He glanced at my wife. "Even you Americans! I'll see you at cocktails at five o'clock?"

Now, as I read rapidly through the news it was clear that the National Socialist Party had first infiltrated the police, then the lower echelons of government and even the "untouchable" trade unions. Rebellion had meant jail at the hands of the S.A. Stormtroopers and one by one they had all succumbed. The Social Democratic Party, whose strength lay in the trade unions, had been banned as an enemy of the people and the state; all the smaller parties had toppled one by one and police occupied their head-quarters and branches.

I felt shocked as I read each item, unemotionally reported. Suddenly, it seemed, democracy in Germany was no more. There had been skirmishes, but tragically a lack of any united opposition, any great leaders, dependable parties or strong national purpose among a war-weary people.

I was startled from my reverie by Dorothy's gentle touch. The customs inspection was complete and we must dash across Bremen to catch the International Express leaving for Prague. I loved this famous train with its cosmopolitan collection of passengers – diplomats with their briefcases, Indian students from Oxford, an occasional Japanese in somber clothes, flanked by a heavy-set Dutch businessman and a solemn pilgrim bound for Mecca.

Today I was happy to find that we had a compartment to ourselves for the first stage of our journey and I could forget my concerns as I shared with Dorothy her fascination with the passing scene – her delight at ancient stone walls in place of barbed wire, Gothic steeples even in the smallest towns, and the solid rounded baroque turrets above the homes of wealthy landowners. As we neared Hanover, the countryside changed; neat, unadorned workers' houses clustered around small new factories.

Then, as the train drew into the station and we stepped out for some fresh air, Dorothy and I walked abruptly into the new reality of German life. Among the motley throng on the platform were groups of fresh-faced young men crisply clad in grey-blue uniforms, laughing and kidding one another uproariously. Suddenly sharp commands rang out above the noise and instantly formations of youth stood at attention, faces wiped clean of expression, then moved in perfect precision, oblivious of the crowds.

I looked intently at those faces and thought each seemed a replica of the others, an absorbed gleam in the eye, but a total unawareness of the human beings around them. This was certainly a very different Germany from the one I knew when I was a student ten years before at Halle in Saxony. At that time I had sensed among the young a gentler, even a subdued spirit. Now that mood, which was perhaps the reflection of confusion and frustration, had given way to an explosion of pride and assertiveness. What had happened to those tender seeds of democracy which we had hoped would thrive in Germany after a rapacious Kaiser was booted out?

I understood all too well as an Austrian that the German respect for order, rank and obedience had been reimposed. And as I watched the uniformed youth making their way towards their destination, oblivious of the people around them, I wondered whether this was a portent of the behavior of a new Germany.

My wife expressed my sentiments more bluntly. She'd just been brushed aside by two marching stormtroopers who seemed not to notice her: "This lot is more concerned about where they're going than with anyone who may stand in their way."

When we re-entered our compartment we found some interesting additions to our company. A distinguished looking Englishman had claimed the seat next to ours and was buried behind *The Times*. Opposite him was a French "doll," highly scented and painted, her costume up where it should have been down, and down where it might better have been up. In the corner opposite us sat a disheveled Yugoslav, talking to a young Czech. Along the corridor outside our compartment others, including a conspicuous group of young Americans, stood laughing and holding hands.

As we picked up speed through tranquil green meadow land the French girl suddenly spoke up loudly in English. "It's awful to see all these young men marching! It's very dangerous for France. My country's suffered so much. My mother and grandmother in all those awful black clothes!" She waved her hands and I noticed that in spite of the brightened nails they were tough and worn. Poor child, much of the land work must have been hers.

The Englishman raised one eye above his newspaper. "A barbaric exhibition! Utterly ridiculous. Can't last." He retreated once more into *The Times*. The Czech was scowling and surprised me by breaking into English. "I cannot look at these Germans. Always they are right! Always they are better than anyone else. They make me sick!" His round peasant face was red with fury and hatred. The young Yugoslav finally turned from the window and said slowly in excellent English, "I think those young men are building up to be a real force. After all, their way of life is certainly better than the soft and selfish 'democracy' I've been seeing in the West. That's a fake. Who knows? Theirs may turn out to be the way of true revolution."

The French girl sat up and hissed, "A Communist! I knew it!" She folded her arms across her chest and closed her eyes. The Yugoslav shrugged and gazed out the window. The Czech looked scandalized that the Yugoslav should have anything good to say about a German. He himself had probably suffered too long at the hands of us Austrians and Germans. Having made their comments on the German scene the company lapsed into prolonged silence. I wondered if their feelings represented those of most of their fellow countrymen.

Dorothy pressed my arm and whispered, "I'm really glad we couldn't bring Jerry. It's all too scary."

Jerry was our nine-month-old baby. My parents had looked forward to meeting him. Someday their ten-thousand-acre estate, with its castles, woods, fields and lakes would be his. But the doctor had said he must not travel and we had left him with Dorothy's parents in San Francisco. I thought longingly of his golden curly head and fat little legs and as Dorothy and our fellow passengers fell asleep in the darkness visions of my years in America chased through my mind. There I had met and married my wife, daughter of several generations of Kentucky planters.

From our attractive San Francisco apartment we could look across the Bay, a magnificent view. I pictured our small damp garden squeezed between our house and a rocky hill behind it. A little green frog lived in our old stone fountain and croaked his heart out unfailingly as dusk fell. In our kitchen, doing his best to cook a meal while warming Jerry's bottle, Louis, our Creole houseboy, quietly worked away. A peaceful and indestructible world. And yet, was it? We and our friends were "sitting pretty," but now this revelation of Hitler's Germany had made me very conscious of what I had known in my head – all around us in the world it was a time of social upheaval and revulsion against injustices.

Even in America all was not as peaceful and prosperous as we would have liked to believe. I had crossed the Atlantic five years earlier, drawn by a conviction that the American way was the right one: racial, cultural and religious minorities living side by side in common commitment to a nation; the breakdown of the rigid class system of Europe; the right of every individual to make his own way. Here was the means by which to lessen the hatred and the endless fears that were tearing apart my own beloved homeland. To me the American ideals carried the fresh impetus the old world needed to lift it into a very different future.

But I found that Americans were having to face their own problems. The Market had fallen, followed by the Great Depression. President Roosevelt had just launched the New Deal. Centralization and socialization through government were being bemoaned by our friends, most of whom belonged to the Social Register crowd of junior executives. They were the country's young leaders, but they were entangled in their own problems and enjoyments.

On a larger scale America was involved with its own affairs, few feeling responsibility for anything beyond its borders. I, too, had been immersed in my family, home, circle of friends and bright prospects for the future. And yet, below my effervescence lay a gnawing consciousness that the world was edging towards catastrophe, and it was all too easy to blame the Red Shirts and Brown Shirts overseas.

With my European background I had been invited from time to time to speak to fairly large groups such as the League against War and Fascism. I gave them what knowledge I possessed – for the most part theories. I was somewhat dismayed to find my audiences made up largely of dewy-eyed older ladies who had taken luxury trips to Europe and on the other hand of rebellious younger people who liked to pitch their theories against mine. Usually I received enough adulation to feel I'd done something for peace.

This bubble had been pricked when I was introduced one day to the author, Anna Louise Strong. She lived up to her name, with a firm square face, short grey hair and cool grey eyes. She was regarded as "very pink," if not a convinced Communist. However, I thought of myself as "very liberal." I started telling her animatedly about my ideas and she listened patiently for a few minutes. Then abruptly, but kindly, she put a hand on my arm and said, "You are interesting, but I must go and finish reading my papers now." Turning on her unfashionable square heels, she walked away.

Sitting now in the railroad compartment my hand strayed to two letters I was carrying in my breast pocket. I knew both of them almost by heart. The first was from my father, offering to pay for our passages so that the parents might get to meet their daughter-in-law. Papa also wrote that he and my brother, Mani, needed my presence because there were many problems to be settled on our Křižanov estates.

Křižanov! How I loved it. I had studied every smallest corner of its ten thousand acres – its gently swelling plains of highest class wheat, its hills of fir and pine and its fifty shimmering lakes stocked with fish. It was for the nurture of these treasures that I had taken my Doctorate in Agriculture. And for the care of the two factories and the general management of a large staff of employees I had taken a Doctorate in Law and in Economics. Beyond all that was the beautiful historic old castle of Křižanov, "Place of the Cross," standing on a slight rise above the little community to which it gave its name, one of the thirteen villages encompassed by our estates.

The second letter I was carrying was from Kubelík, the general manager of the estates. He had written:

"There are many changes to report here with us as well as in the whole economic situation in the country. These require careful consideration. You may be assured that we all think of you much more than you probably imagine and we hope that in your mutual love and respect you are finding compensation for the storm which today is shaking humanity to the roots. We are actually facing a materialism so strong that humanity is being driven towards complete ruin....

"One can well understand the difficult situation in which His Grace, your father, finds himself. He urgently needs support from one of his own blood and who else should that be but you? His Grace has changed in many ways, so he seems easier on us all than we were used to in the past. Their Lordships seem lonesome and they have every right to feel that way, especially in these difficult times of which the end is not in sight."

The letter touched me deeply. Kubelík was the man who had gently led me as a youth through the maze of responsibilities I would one day assume. As the wheels of the train clicked evenly on the tracks my mind slid back to the past with a clarity so often obscured by the tensions of my life in America, where I had tended to live in the grip of the immediate decisions of the moment. I pictured K, who was also Head Forester, taking me by the hand, a nine-year-old clad in my inevitable Austrian knit grey sweater bordered in green, and my *Lederhosen,* far up into the dark woods following trails known only to the deer and to him. As the moon sank below the horizon some heightened instinct kept him moving at his unhurried pace without stumbling through the velvet darkness. The crackling of a misplaced footstep could send the deer leaping headlong through the bushes. I would wince as my bare knees caught in the brambles, but not the slightest whimper was allowed.

At last we would reach the small look-out hut with its view of the whole valley. There, wrapped in a heavy blanket, with my pad pulled close to K's, I slept soundly until, in the first grey light of morning, his gentle hand shook me. Then we stood motionless side by side until full light burst suddenly upon us and we saw a magnificent stag, heavy antlers raised proudly as he nibbled the soft green leaves. At the edge of a blue lake below us the doe sipped at the water, two speckled fawns beside her wobbling on their delicate legs. Then, as I watched breathlessly, they played games together, nudging and shoving, leaping and running, flicking one another with a tiny hoof, until the dew began to dry from the meadow. Then, like shadows, they slid into the bushes.

My heart had swelled with love for these beautiful animals as I watched them in their home and I would look up at K with my eyes full of wonder. He would smile down at me in silent understanding. Then we would slip away to his small hut in the depth of the forest to sit down to his wife's steaming porridge, milk, honey and the best Czech dumplings. Her first question was always, "How many points did he have on his antlers?" It was K's job to know the habits, the ages and number of points, as well as the usual whereabouts of these stag, so that when the stag shooting season came he could lead Papa and his guests – we called them "guns" – unerringly to their locale.

Despite K's love for these animals there was no false sentimentality about him. All year until the shooting season he could care for them, but knew the exact number that then must be killed in order that the balance of nature could be maintained.

It was Papa who taught me at the age of twelve to shoot. This gentleman's sport also had its unbreakable rules. I vividly recalled the day when I shot my final exact bull's eye on the target. Dressed in my full shooting regalia – grey-green plus fours, hand-knitted stockings to match, and wide-lapelled suede jacket, I then leaned casually against a tree, my hand resting on the muzzle of my gun, waiting for praise from Papa. Instead, he walked over and quietly removed my hand from the muzzle and took the gun from me. "You may have your gun in six months, son," he said sternly.

"But, Papa, the gun was empty."

"You have broken the first law of hunting. You know that no huntsman ever places a hand on a muzzle – regardless." And he walked away. It was six months to the day before I saw the gun again. And I would never forget the lesson.

The truth was, I admitted to myself, as the first lights of Prague now appeared through the windows, that I had left home for America, dazzled by its call to freedom and democracy, in search of adventure and of course to make a fortune, but primarily to escape for a time from Papa's discipline and the demands and responsibilities of an ancestral estate. I had wanted to be master of my own fate, stand on my own feet, run my own business. And I'd made a moderate but promising start at that.

The conductor thrust his head into the compartment, called "Praha!" and handed each our passport, then slammed the door. "Zlatá Praha!" – Golden Prague! The station lights shone dimly in the gloom of the small hours. We manhandled our luggage through the windows to the porters, who trundled them to the customs. Dorothy and I caught a short sleep at a small hotel before the next stretch of our journey to Brunn (Brno).

We were not the only early passengers on the small train. Farmers and their wives and children and chickens and geese crowded into the third-class compartment. We gratefully grabbed the *Schinkensemmel* – pink ham piled into fresh buns – and mugs of steaming coffee on sale and wedged ourselves on the hard wood seats between the peasants and cages of squawking chickens. The windows were tight closed and the aroma of hot humanity was rising. I reached over and raised a window. Immediately, without expression, one of the women closed it tight again. The fowl, it seemed, did not like cool early morning air. I caught Dorothy's eye. Trapped between stout farming wives, she was doing her best to refrain from laughter and from holding her nose.

Soon she was uttering "ohs" and "aahs" as she gazed out at the Bohemian landscape so familiar to me – lush green grass, hillsides climbing easily to the edge of dark pine forests. We passed close by a small pool where three deer and their tiny fawns were drinking the fresh morning water. As our train clacked noisily by they raised their heads, quiet and unconcerned.

"This is a different world from Germany," she said. I nodded. Now we were passing a field golden with wheat, then oats and sugar beets, all waving in the light summer breeze. "Das ist Korn," I told her loudly, "und das ist Hafer und Weizen." The farmers were as surpised as was Dot. My city-bred wife didn't know the difference between grain in any language. But it was a lesson important to be learned before meeting my family. I heard her muttering after me in her American-German "wheat, potatoes, oats, sugarbeets." Then I taught her the names of pines and firs as we passed the forests.

As the train came into Brno station I leaned out the window and made out two figures frantically waving – brother Mani and his wife Alice, here to drive us the hour-long trip to Křižanov. Mani, two years younger than I, was my only brother. Since our days together in Jesuit school we had been very close. Here he was, complete with his shooting hat, decorated with the emblems of Moravian and Hungarian estates, each awarded to distinguished huntsmen at their shoots and to desirable guests. Like Papa, Mani was one of the best shots in the land, well liked, full of charm, good humor and kind almost to a fault.

After we untangled ourselves from their embraces, Mani grinned, "So you've finally both come to eat your *Knedlíček* (Czech dumpling) and *Sauerkraut*!" He turned to Dorothy, "But I bet he didn't tell you you'd hate their taste!"

Mani wagged his finger in mock severity. "You are fourteen minutes and twenty seconds late, and Papa won't approve of that, especially as half the village will be streaming to the castle for the 'bit of a greeting' they've been preparing all week. Of course Mama won't mind – she'll be late, too."

He kept up his running banter as we collected our luggage. Outside the station Franta Karmazín was awaiting us, his leather leggings gleaming, his chauffeur's cap in hand. Karmazín was an important personality in our household and I greeted him warmly and presented him to Dot. Big, strong and blond, he spoke German well. We set off, with Mani driving us in Papa's big Tatra and Karmazín following with the luggage in Mani's small car.

Mani drove rapidly and well, punctuating his questions with airy waves of his hand in the Austrian manner as we rolled through villages with small whitewashed or pastel-colored cottages, with their thatched roofs. Each had its characteristic mark, a brilliant geranium in a single window, framed in dark blue, or a purple petunia framed in white.

In the fields women in full blue skirts and kerchiefs tied under their chins worked steadily, swinging their scythes as ably as the men beside them. We could hear them singing in harmony the folk songs of the country. The tunes were often picked up by older men and women driving their horse-drawn, heavily laden wagons and ox carts over the rough roads. All seemed to be sharing in the joy of harvest time. Scantily clad and naked children played in the village streets, splashing in the puddles or herding chickens and geese ahead of them.

Around a last gentle curve stood the village of Křižanov, a little larger than the other dozen villages on our land. Its houses were placed at a respectful distance from the wall behind which lay the lovely park around the castle. Our car stopped at the park's entrance. I heard Dorothy's gasp as she stared up at an arch framing the grilled iron gates. Intricately woven roses, carnations, daisies, violets and petunias spelled out in red, white and blue the greeting "Wilkommen." Beneath it stood a group of townspeople, dressed in their colorful best, smiling broadly as they greeted us.

We stepped out of the car as two tiny children thrust out to my wife yellow field flowers, then rushed back shyly to their mother's skirts. Dot was speechless, tears in her eyes as she bent to receive the bouquets. Then came the men with a hearty welcome, shaking my hand and kissing Dorothy's as I presented her to them. We thanked them all with full hearts, as Mani and Alice looked on beaming.

We drove on through the park to the castle, whose gates were opened smoothly by two liveried footmen and we were in the four-square courtyard. Its spacious and ageless beauty struck me afresh, its two tiers of stately Roman arches, so perfectly designed and dating back to the days when Křižanov had been a Benedictine monastery; the massive stag heads mounted on the wall between and behind each archway, each head labeled with its history and the prowess of its hunter. And Mama's final touch – between each arch a huge stone urn from which geraniums spilled profusely over the balustrade.

At the foot of the stone steps leading into the castle stood Mama and Papa, backed by the house staff of twenty-eight, each standing stiffly – the butler, house servants and maids in their uniforms. I took Dorothy by the hand as Mama stepped forward, a moment never to be forgotten. Mama took Dorothy in her arms as tears slipped down her face. Then, holding her at arms' length to see her better, she

smiled up at the pretty young face, noted the chic traveling costume, well made shoes, slender and delicate hands.
"You look Austrian!" And that, I knew was the ultimate
accolade.

Next came Papa, gruff and moved, to give her a hearty
hug, hold both hands and kiss them. In turn, each of the
servants was presented, to kiss her hand while warmly con-
gratulating me. And so my American wife began the
conquest of her Austrian family.

Mama saw the weariness in Dorothy's face and led us to
our suite which she had tastefully prepared. A large
canopied bed dominated the bedroom, with intricately
carved wardrobes around the walls. We had separate dress-
ing rooms, an enormous bath and a charming drawing room
looking out over a small lake in the park. Mama was
obviously hoping for a long visit.

There to greet me was my valet, an old friend. For Dot
there was a maid, a new girl who stammered a few words
in broken German and was relieved when I replied in
Czech. She busied herself unpacking Dot's evening clothes
while Dot luxuriated in a steaming bath. Suddenly I heard
a plaintive "Gene!" My wife, swathed in a huge bath towel,
was sitting on the edge of the bed, with the maid kneeling
at her feet with a pair of stockings in her hands. "Gene,
I can't make her understand I can put on my stockings by
myself."

"Of course you can, darling, but you don't want to hurt
her pride. This is probably her first job at the castle and she's
scared of failing."

Dot doubtfully stuck out a leg. Finally she appeared in
a lovely rose chiffon dress and we made our way down to
join the family awaiting us in the formal salon. Dot murmured in my ear, "It's as big as our whole apartment."

With Mama and Papa, Mani and Alice was cousin Willy,
Papa's nephew, a pleasant soul who had been wounded
in the war and now gave the nonchalant appearance that
nothing more was expected of him from life.

"This is a gorgeous room, Mama," said Dorothy.

"See," I said, pointing to the shining parquet floor, "this is hand-laid and the ceiling is quite famous because it's hand plastered with those arabesques and garlands." Mama had hung blue silk drapes in each deeply cut window recess, along with blue, rose and white hydrangeas. Around the fireplace were French style settees and damask and tapestried chairs. Prominent on one wall was a painting by Lazlo of Mama, slim-waisted and ruffled and a huge garden hat tilted becomingly on her head, with me, a child of four, clad in white satin breeches, still with shoulder length golden curls.

At 8.30 sharp, dinner was announced. Papa led my wife into the dining room, with Mama on my arm and the others trailing. The white damask table cover gleamed under the low hanging crystal chandelier. At each place was a silver plate – a gift from neighbors and friends for my parents' silver wedding anniversary. There were seventy of them and guests enjoyed looking to see whose name and crest was emblazoned on the bottom. In the center of the table stood a hand-cut crystal epergne artistically arranged by Miroush, head butler, in an intricate design of roses, violets, glazed green leaves and ferns from the hot house. I saw him furtively watching for my wife's reaction as he and two footmen held the ladies' chairs. Papa was at his most gracious best and enjoyed Dorothy sampling her first roebuck and the chocolate soufflé prepared by Rosa, who lived up to her reputation as the best cook in Moravia.

At first the conversation was a little uneven since Mama's belief that her French was the equal of my wife's proved unfounded. When Mama faltered for a French word she would return to her comfortable German. I did my best with my interpretation to bridge the differences between cultures and continents. One simple question asked of my wife that evening has gone down in our family's history. Mama, who could not cook, but knew just how each dish should taste, turned to Dorothy. "We must have some of your American dishes for you, if you will tell Rosa how to make them."

Dorothy looked at me in panic as I translated. I knew she could neither cook, nor train a cook. Then she smiled; "Well," she said brightly, "I think pineapple and cottage cheese salad is one of our best recipes." She was sure she could handle that; pineapple came out of a can, mayonnaise out of a jar and cottage cheese out of a container. But Mama looked startled. "Well, we will ask the gardener tomorrow if the pineapples are ripe in the hot houses. Mayonnaise.." Mama was struggling to be polite. "Do Americans put mayonnaise on fruit?"

I groaned inwardly. First law of French cuisine already broken! And canned pineapple! But I really suffered when Dot attempted to describe cottage cheese and I tried to interpret. Confusion grew deeper until Alice chimed in, "Oh, I know what it must be – goat's milk all churned up into – uh – clots. Very popular in Italy."

Two days later a not quite ripe pineapple appeared on the table beautifully decorated with very green lettuce upon which sat a large pile of goat's milk, churned and in curds – tasting and smelling very obviously of its origin. The home-made mayonnaise was arranged in a star pattern on the side. Rosa had done her best, but it was almost inedible.

Fortunately this evening Papa embarked on a lively conversation about this year's harvest. Dot, grasping that the topic was crops, spoke up charmingly, "Oh, ja, dass war die Weisen, die Hafer and die, er, das Korn." Papa roared with laughter and rose delightedly to kiss her.

The servants removed the finger bowls and it was time for the toasts. Papa rose with his usual dignity and with real warmth, helped a little by the champagne and customary Austrian sentiment, toasted his new daughter-in-law. Nor did he forget his grandchild, eventual heir, Eugene III (Jerry). Then came Mani, brief, amusing and droll. My wife sat at ease, face glowing. Lastly, I responded with a sense of happy fulfillment. This was the acceptance for

which I had longed. My wife, my family and my country
– my three loves together. The future would be glorious.
It was, but not at all in the manner I had envisaged.

2

Papa

DOROTHY AND I sat chatting with Mama, Papa and Willy over a leisurely breakfast. This in itself was an unusual occasion since Mama had taken to having her breakfast in bed to avoid Papa's annoyance at her constant unpunctuality. Mani and Alice sauntered in and made the rounds, kissing or shaking hands according to station and sex. Mani, still a dutiful son after 29 years, leaned over Papa's hand, kissing it as well as his cheek. I had done my best to prepare my wife for these strict Austrian customs and to my amusement I watched her pushing her hand dutifully towards any male who approached her, sometimes having to withdraw it hurriedly when she realized he was a passing waiter or porter.

''Such a beautiful day,'' ventured Mani; ''Alice and I thought we might abduct Dorothy and Gene for lunch at our place and possibly drive up to Pernštejn later. That is of course if our parents consent.''

Mama's knitted brows and ominous silence from Papa hinted that parental consent would not be forthcoming. Back to normal in the family, I thought wryly. Blissfully unconscious of the tension, Dot started to accept enthusiastically, when Mama burst out, ''*Well*, I had thought to show Dorothy around the park and fruit and vegetable gardens, but of course it's up to her.'' She rose majestically, calling to her three dogs, Negus, Tupfi and Hexe and stood regally at the high arched French doors. ''If anyone wants to come along, fine. Otherwise I'll go alone with the dogs. We don't mind, do we, Tupfi?''

Unmoved, Papa spoke peremptorily: ''You will no doubt

remember, Mani, that I called a conference for nine o'clock this morning with the estate manager and all the foresters. It's now ten to nine. We must decide quickly what we do afterwards.''

This drew a sharp retort from Mama. ''Eugene, why do you always have to plan these conferences just when we have something else to do? Sometimes I wonder if you do it deliberately!''

''My dear, how could we carry out these impractical plans of yours without the money from a properly managed estate? I realize you have very little knowledge of . . .''

''The money you and your managers plan on spending!'' Mama's voice was shrill.

''The money from the lakes, farms and woods which enables us to live adequately,'' Papa responded angrily. ''Money without which you'd have to do without your guests, your fancy gardens and your theater.''

This exchange was obviously one that had occurred many times before. Mama knew when she was beaten. ''I didn't expect you'd understand.''

''My sons will come with me. Dorothy and Alice can accompany you and the dogs in the park.''

Neither Dorothy's nor my wishes had been consulted. I'd been looking forward to showing her Pernštejn, an historic castle belonging to Alice's family. But this was no time for more argument. Papa was already talking to the three men-servants who had served breakfast, telling them the numbers expected for luncheon and dinner. He added, ''Of course you and the kitchen will hold yourselves in readiness for several of their lordships in the neighborhood dropping in for tea. They may stay for dinner. Some of them maybe overnight. Miruš, I'll tell you later which wines to serve for dinner.''

Telephones were still an uncertain means of communication in our countryside, so the domestic staff had to be prepared for any number of guests anytime. In the summertime unexpected guests were no problem, but our extremely

cold winters required a day's warning so that guest
suites could be heated, and with ninety-nine rooms in
the castle that was no small matter. Nevertheless, between
neighboring castles hospitality was boundless – invitations
were never required, only announcements of one's
arrival.

Papa consulted his gold Swiss chronometer. "Almost
nine," and headed in his measured pace to the main office,
followed by Mani and me. He entered the heavily vaulted
room with a crisp "Guten Morgen" and a "Hunters' Heil,"
the salutation used among foresters and game keepers. All
rose with a shuffle of sturdy boots and a chorus of "Hunter's
Heils" and "Good day, Gracious Sir." I shook hands with
each of the men, most of whom had been friends since my
childhood.

Chief Forester Panák was on his feet to give his precise
report. Tall and gaunt, he had worked with Papa ever since
Papa had inherited the estate some forty years ago. He had
taught Mani and me the ways of the forest and the strict
code of a hunter. Then he turned to me. "Well, young sir,
you really are a man now! Why didn't you bring your son
with you? A little forest air would do him good, too. That
city air you left him in is no good!"

Panak was the one man permitted a jest in Papa's
presence. Papa was beaming. Next came Kubelík, Director
of the estate, the friend who had written to me to remind
me of my responsibilities to my father, and I thanked him
for it. "Our Gracious Sir and Her Grace must be glad to
have you here," he replied. "We all need you." Kubelík
was followed by Forester Nederly, stern looking, with his
clear eyes and clay pipe clamped firmly beneath his bushy
mustache. He ruled the village and district of Sklenny, in
the furthest reaches of the estate, with a tyrant's discipline.
I put my hand on his arm. "Do you remember, Mr. Forester,
how you wouldn't allow us even a quiet cough when we
were stalking?"

"Of course not, Sir Doctor, but I always allowed you two

or three minutes for coughing when I knew the deer or blackcock were not on hand."

"Are you still waking the hunters with your bugle call at 4 a.m.? And does Mrs. Forester still serve that wonderful thick cream in the morning coffee?"

With a twitch of his formidable mustache Nederly answered gloomily, "Times have changed. Not as many blackcocks, and their Lordships don't stay with us overnight anymore." He glanced at Papa; "Sir Count came last time early in the morning in his fast car. But not quite early enough and we had to hurry through the woods and some scared the game by stepping on branches. No, it's not the same."

Papa frowned and Mani gave me a wink.

The last forester in line was a new man, Zyp, who managed the sawmill. "It's rough going," he said. "Storms and hoar-frost have brought down so many trees, but what's worse is the Depression. We have so much beautiful lumber on hand, but often can't sell it at a profit." Mani had told me that in spite of Papa's excellent management of the estate the bankers were breathing down his neck. He hated dealing with bankers and I foresaw that such would soon be my lot.

We moved from the Foresters to the Fishmaster, a ruggedly built young man who had brought the fisheries to a yearly yield of three to five hundred tons of highly-prized rainbow trout, pike and carp. They fetched the best price in the markets of Brno, our Moravian capital. Toník was the one man in the estate council with whom we spoke Czech – with all the others it was German, even though they were Czechs. Papa was not fluent in Czech and no government regulations or anything else would shift him from his ways. Mama had never been able to master the language, Mani and I of the younger generation spoke it well and without accent.

Toník forecast a good fish harvest this year and promised me a fishing day in Podhrasky, the lake below the castle, "such as you have never seen before. They are fat, their snouts are short. They are beauties."

I looked with interest at the next man in line, the young manager of the distillery in which potatoes and corn produced industrial alcohol. Papa had built the plant, but in the land reform of 1918 it had been expropriated and turned over to a cooperative of peasants and landowners. Papa still held a majority of the shares and was entrusted with its operation. The young manager was respectful but clearly felt responsible to the community rather than to our family. He was no longer part of the "old order."

Last in line was Forester John J, who had started service in the family as Papa's personal valet, then studied forestry and emerged as the most reliable forester with a good head, heart and humor. His head was always cocked at an angle and he had a comical habit of shifting his weight from one foot to another. He had caused great comment in the community by bringing into his home a young widow and the two had lived together and raised a family without benefit of clergy. She had a good pension from her first marriage, so "why lose that when we can live together loyally without marriage?"

John J's attitude towards religion was typical of that shared by most of these men of fields and forests. Most never darkened a church door except for a funeral, when they dressed in their best to celebrate the occasion. Religion was all right for their wives, they said, and of course for the lords of the manors. For them, the liberal, partly educated new bourgeois class, religion was a matter of the past. They remained good friends with the priest, who played cards with them over a glass of beer in the village inn in the hope of winning their souls, but rarely succeeded.

John J. now started a lively debate with Forester Nederly by inviting me to go stalking with him, "We have some good bucks this year, one with eight points, and I have a high stand all set up on Odonen Meadow." Nederly interrupted impatiently, "Young Sir, Sir Doctor, I still have one

capital buck that comes out every night like clockwork, but
the grain is growing high and soon you won't be able to
see him.'' As the two men stepped up their argument Papa
had to interrupt, promising that I would visit both their
districts.

"Now, let us go into the forestry office,'' he decreed
abruptly and walked ahead of us through the finance office
into a large conference room, double vaulted with star-like
arches. Two windows, cut into the five-foot thick outer
walls, let in a pale light illuminating whitewashed walls and
a great, heavy armoire filled with old maps and records of
the estate. Current maps covered each wall. Papa made for
a massive desk at which he seated himself, leaving the rest
of us to sit or stand – only the Director, the four Foresters,
the Fishmaster, Mani and I were expected at this meeting.
Everything was conducted with strict protocol. This was the
time for the detailed reports from the forests, sawmill and
fish ponds, followed by an estimate of the shooting situation. Agricultural matters were covered only by father and
the Director. The one department that was not discussed
at all was finances; this Papa took care of by himself, the
one flaw in his management.

"We'll begin with the Sklenny District," said Papa and
turned to me. ''That's the one worst hit by heavy winds
and hoar-frost. How is it going, Nederly? Have you found
any bark beetles?''

Nederly burst out excitedly, ''Your Gracious Sir, I just
cannot get enough people. In the old days I could round
up men, or have them send their wives. I told them if they
didn't come they'd get no roots or wood for their winter
fires. But nowadays they don't listen to me anymore!'' .

Mani quietly suggested that Nederly might get further
with reasoning than threats, but the Forester retorted that
there were too many smart-alecs among the young. Trying
to reason with them simply undercut his authority. Zyp,
in charge of the sawmill, chimed in that he had the same
trouble there. Papa was clearly becoming impatient with

the way the talk was going. He wanted to know exactly how many men and women in each preserve were being employed in reforesting, cutting out dead trees and working on the lumber brought down in last year's storm.

The numbers listed by Nederly were clearly inadequate. He ended by saying that the search for the destructive bark beetles had produced seven of them. Papa smiled: "Well, you still have a few more workers than beetles! But we must see that the beetles don't catch up with you. We might have to bring in some work gangs from Slovakia." He turned to Kubelík: "Are you getting a gang leader to bring in a gang for the field harvest?"

Kubelík said he had ordered one, and Papa told him to ask for another hundred men to work in the forests and the sawmill. There was a moment of silence and then John J. said firmly, "There is a good deal of feeling now, Gracious Sir, between our Moravian Czechs and the Slovaks. I would rather try to get along with just our own people."

The Chief Forester nodded in agreement, but Nederly, rolling his eyes and twirling his mustache, firmly disagreed. "I most certainly need those Slovaks, Your Grace, to do what needs to be done." Papa asked where he would house them and Nederly said that in the summer he would put them in the forestry shed and stables. "Our wives can cook for them," he added. "Beans and potatoes with an occasional bit of boiled beef or sausage are all they ask, provided we give them some schnapps on Sunday."

"Zyp, can you house them in the sawmill?"

"We'll empty two large offices and engage a girl to cook for them, Your Grace. The only trouble is I'll have to train them, and those simple-minded Slovaks aren't easy to train."

Oh, oh! I said to myself. Here's that national superiority again. It's not only in us Austrians, it's just as strong in the Czechs. Father was starting to move on to the detailed reports from the preserves when I was startled by a firm nudge from Mani, sitting beside me. "As usual," he whispered fiercely, "Papa hasn't time for these 'irrelevant' issues of housing and care for our employees. And their complaints never reach him."

"Then why don't you bring them up with him?"

Mani silently shrugged his shoulders and gave me a long look. We both knew the answer. At that moment it was crystal clear to me that if anyone were to stand up to Papa and try to edge him from his feudal world into the realities of today's more democratic society it would have to be me. I did not relish the idea.

3

Mama

MAMA'S VOICE floated up through the open window. She was showing off the formal garden to Dorothy. Pointing with her walking stick to the green hedges trimmed into gracious star designs enclosing the rose beds. "I've done all this during the past year," she was saying. "When I found all those lovely baroque statues I had this terracing done to give them the right setting. There's so much I still want to do, but there's always that dratted money question. There never seems to be enough to make my beautiful dreams come true!"

"The eternal complaint of us all," Dorothy laughed. "But your dreams have already produced a lovely entrance."

Mama, I thought, had always disdained money matters. Well born, with a goodly fortune of her own, she had never had to ask a price or pay a bill for anything until she married Papa, whose family tree and fortune were considerably less lofty than hers. It had been a love match at the start, and when the adjustment period began the extraordinary respect and affection that Papa seemed to draw to himself somehow bridged the widening disagreements.

Alice and Willy had joined them. "Mama, do show Dorothy what else you're doing." Thus encouraged, Mama moved off to the wing that jutted out from the right side of the castle. Formerly a brewery, it had been her *bête noire*.

"Look," she said triumphantly, "behind these ugly vines that are supposed to hide the building and under that thick whitewash I discovered this beautiful early seventeenth century *sgraffito* work. I had some art experts lay it bare." She sounded a little defensive as she went on, "Of course we had to pay the craftsmen plenty, but it wasn't too expensive when you realize that this is the first thing you see as you approach the castle."

They wandered out of earshot, but Mama had stirred my memories. I leaned across the deep window-sill and looked down to where an ancient lime tree had once spread its branches, shading this side wall. Three hundred years old, it had seemed to Mani and me an indestructible giant. Then, during a storm one night, it fell with a horrendous crash. Next morning we walked around its sprawling limbs, split and broken. It seemed to my young mind an omen of a world breaking apart.

Shortly afterwards the storms of the First World War had felled that seemingly invincible structure, the Austro-Hungarian empire. Memories of the shock I had experienced could still bring a cold sweat as I relived the shambles of an uprooted society. But with the resilience of a sixteen-year-old I had moved into the new age and assumed that it would inevitably spell progress. My parents were of a different mind. Tomás Masaryk had carved an independent nation, Czechoslovakia, out of that empire, incorporating Moravia with our estates into his territory, but for Papa and Mama their life-style would continue as best it might.

Mani arrived to interrupt my reveries and we joined our wives to find Mama launched into one of her favorite subjects. She was waving a hand around our Renaissance courtyard: "One must demand honesty in buildings as well as in humans. You have to lay bare the beautiful lines and materials. Willy can tell you how I fought to have the vines removed to reveal these graceful columns and capitals."

Mani, obviously tired of this philosophizing interjected, "But don't you think, Mama, we should consider more seriously how to improve the living conditions of the families in this part of the building?"

Alice slipped quietly behind her husband, fearful of Mama's reaction. Dorothy, unaware of any danger, plunged in, ''Yes, I would really like to see some of the apartments – just how employees live and work. And maybe, Gene, we could visit some of the homes in the village. The houses are so lovely, with their fresh paint and attractive colors.''

Now even Mani was looking a little disconcerted, but Dot went on unperturbed, ''I was struck by what you said, Mama, about honesty in buildings as well as in people. Did you mean, Mani, that to make the buildings really honest the apartments need to be straightened up?'' She stared at the dark brewery wing: ''I suppose that with no sunshine on this side these are the bathrooms and kitchens?''

I laughed inwardly. Thank God for my American wife; fearless or naive, she was launching us into reality!

After a moment of tense silence Mama sputtered, ''What nonsense you brought up, Mani. How would I know what their apartments are like? I have no idea how many of them have bathrooms. I know the director has one. Anyway, they are accustomed to whatever they have. At least they never say anything.''

Mani's face was now red with anger. This was a sore subject with him: ''The truth is that some of these apartments are certainly not in good condition. Most of them have no bathrooms and some people have to use outhouses, even in winter.''

Now Mama was embarrassed. She turned to Dorothy: ''When I first came to Křižanov I tried hard to get to know people in the village, to visit them and help with their babies and children. I was impressed like you with their pretty cottages, but I was shocked with how dirty the children were, rolling in the dust and running around in bare feet, even with well-to-do parents. I wanted to teach them hygiene; I couldn't speak their tongue, but I took along my Czech maid.''

Mama shook her head: ''The stench in some of those homes! I really did try hard, but do you know what I got in return for my trouble? I was resented. Oh, of course they would bow and kiss my hand, but when I asked about their children and offered to wash and dress them, they just looked downright sulky. Sometimes they even refused to answer me. I felt that if they didn't want my help, why should I come?'' She looked bewildered and was pleading with Dorothy. For once, Dot said nothing.

"That was in the good old Austrian days,'' Mama went on. ''Now that the Czechs feel they are the masters of creation with all this republican democracy, you can imagine how they would receive any of us in their homes! If I hear one of them is sick or in trouble I try to send something. I also invite them, especially the children, to my marionette theater and they love it. That is something I can put my whole heart into. I even get some of our house girls to take parts in the plays.''

Dorothy, bless her heart, still said nothing, and Mother went on, ''I get along well with the craftsmen I teach to copy my furniture, and with the gardeners. But in all the years I've been here I've never been able to learn their dreadful language – their nouns have seven declensions – absurd! I got into such dreadful arguments with my teacher we both gave up.'' Mama laughed heartily. She had talked herself out of a difficult corner.

Relieved, Alice relinquished her grasp of Mani's arm. He was the usual victim of Mama's tantrums. Somehow Mama seemed to check her temper with me, her firstborn. Maybe it was because I'd learned not to take her too seriously. Now Alice, the perennial peacemaker who always skirted the controversial issues, suggested to Mama that she show Dorothy her theater.

Only too happy to do so, Mama led us to the north wing and into her joy and delight. From perhaps as early as the 13th century half the ground floor of this wing had housed a theater. As a young man Papa had loved to act and to hold theater parties. He had also played the violin, giving recitals on his own Guarnieri. As kids, Mani and I had our own crowd "playing theater.'' Now Mama had converted the already well-equipped legitimate stage into a magnificently appointed marionette theater.

To the right of its entrance Mani pointed out to my wife an impressive five-foot tall coat of arms. It had belonged to the Cistercian monastery, Zdarec Abbey, which had owned our castle until the 18th century. The monastery had been secularized and made part of our family's possession. Mama had created a delicately carved framework for the stage, complete with chubby cherubs swinging golden garlands, and installed some seventy gold and white Louis XV armchairs for the audience.

She took us backstage to examine the intricately constructed puppets, a wonderland of small helmeted knights, romantic ladies, gnomes and a Christmas scene – many made by people from the village. She said she had just managed to finish all this before her money ran out.

Dorothy had stopped before a court jester. "He looks solemn enough for the most subtle jokes!" she exclaimed. "What do you do with these gruesome little gnomes?"

"They are for a play called 'The Forest and Newsprint.' It dramatizes the conflict between Mother Nature – all the inhabitants of the forest – and man's rotten civilization."

Dorothy protested, "Do you feel, Mama, that all civilization is rotten? Surely you wouldn't want to undo it all and go back to primitive times?"

"Of course it's rotten. I dream of earlier ages when life was simpler and more real, before that awful technology ruined our age. Of course I appreciate many conveniences – my bathroom, my comforts, but technology is spoiling everything beautiful, especially the forests. Its machines invade our lives. They've created the age of the masses, the dull grey masses."

Increasingly indignant, she went on to say that people wanted to pull her down to that dull grey level. We must all be democratic, they said. But why should we have to be low and dirty in mind and body and end up being just mediocre? She asked Dorothy and me, coming from one of those so-called democratic countries, didn't we have wealthy and privileged people there? Of course we did. You couldn't make everyone equal. We were not all meant to be equal.

There was no question of my mother's sincerity, and I could see Dorothy didn't know how to answer her. I was about to step in when Mani spoke up loudly, "But Mama, what should we do without technology in . . ."

Alice's clear voice cut in, determined to avoid a familiar confrontation, "Mama, these four lovely white horses must surely be new."

I thought with irritation, she'll smother Mani with her damn protectiveness. Why couldn't she let him fight his own battles?

"Back to reality," said Mani abruptly. "I'm going to show Dorothy the castle from the ground up." He strode across the courtyard and grasped a big iron ring on a heavy trap door resting in the brick floor and lifted one flap. A musty odor rose from the stone steps leading down into darkness.

"The smell of history," he said, playing his flashlight down the steps. "This is the original part of the first castle built in the 11th or 12th century."

"Was it ever a dungeon?" asked Dorothy, whose knowledge of castles began with Byron and ended with Sir Walter Scott.

"Of course," I answered, "but it now houses nothing more formidable than Papa's wines and liquors."

Mani went on to tell her about the two-tiered Renaissance colonnades which extended around the courtyard. Originally the house was only two stories, but Great-Grandfather had too much money, Mani said with a wry smile, and had added the third floor and the clock towers on the three corners. Then he said he'd like to show her the archive room. It contained a relic of the early 15th century such as she'd hardly find anywhere else.

We followed him to a small room tucked away under the stairs outside Papa's office. There, in the back of the room, stood a huge old chalice, four feet high, of noble design with a representation of the host raised above the lid of the cup. As Mani played his light over its surface, what had appeared as silver was revealed as brass that had been zinced over. It glowed like old Sheffield plate. Mani told Dorothy it was more than five hundred years old and had once stood on the flat tower above the chapel.

"It was a symbol of the Hussites," Mani explained. "Jan Hus, one of the first Reformers, was burned at the stake by the Council of Constance in 1415, even though he'd been promised safe passage back to Bohemia. His infuriated followers retaliated against us Catholics by burning 1500 towns and villages here in Bohemia and Moravia. Then the Hussites took over our chapel in the castle."

"What was all the conflict about?" asked Dorothy.

Mani explained that at the heart of it were two differing views of Holy Communion. These were symbolized by the chalice and the cross. The Hussites replaced the cross with the chalice. Later, the Catholics regained control of the region and resubstituted the cross. These hatreds still live on today, he added. "When this chalice fell off the chapel tower during a storm our parents were going to put it back. After all, it had been there two hundred years. But our village priest, usually very peaceful, was deeply upset. He regarded it is an anti-Catholic symbol. The battle divided the district."

Dorothy asked which side won.

"Papa decided to have the chalice hidden away down here and not to replace it with a cross. So the tower may look a little bald, but the controversy died down."

But the trouble was, he added, that beneath the religious issue was a national confrontation. Following the Protestant Reformation the fighting that broke out between the Protestant nobles and the Catholic Habsburgs ended with the defeat of the former by the latter. That was really the defeat of the flower of the Czech national aristocracy by the Austrian rulers. Czechs had lived under the shadow of that ever since.

"I wish they'd taught us these things in school," Dorothy responded. "It would have made it a lot easier to understand what's going on in the world today."

Mani laughed. "We in Czechoslovakia grow up knowing about them, but it doesn't seem to help us too much. Today they're being used to fan hatred between us Austrians and Czechs."

"Yes," I added, "Hitler and Stalin seem to know only too well how to do that."

Our talk was interrupted by a bell that rang out faint but demanding across the courtyard. "That's Mirus," Mani told Dorothy. "It means we have exactly fifteen minutes to prepare for lunch – or risk the terrible wrath of Papa, standing with his watch in hand to confront any latecomer!"

4

The Nobility

THE NEXT FEW DAYS were filled with the social courtesies demanded among the wide circle of friends and relatives of our family. My bride must be paraded among them.

The first engagement was a glorified tea party and tennis tournament given by Alice's brother Vladimír at his home, Rožínka, a typical Moravian castle. But on the way there we were taken by Mani and Alice to visit another legendary castle, Pernštejn, one of the four owned by Alice's father, Count Mittrowsky. On a beautiful July morning Mani drove us along a narrow country lane until around a bend the huge fortress loomed before us, perched on the crest of a heavily wooded hill a mile away. With its many high gables, towers and turrets it would have seemed natural to be met by knights of King Arthur or King Wenceslas riding to meet us. This was a view familiar to millions, since it was embossed on a popular Czech postage stamp.

The lane was the only approach to the castle, whose massive walls sprang straight out of the craggy mountain rocks. We passed over a drawbridge and under the arches of the guard tower into the first courtyard. Before us stood a flight of 180 steps to a second drawbridge behind which stood the massive entrance hall. I remembered the night, some fifteen years earlier, when Alice's sister Isenbeth was married to a young baron from Bohemia. We had arrived in style, pulled by a pair of Papa's fast American trotters. The whole place shimmered under the light of blazing torches held aloft by grooms in hunting livery lining the stairway.

Here it was that Alice and her brothers and sisters had

spent many summers. "We didn't enjoy Pernštejn very much," she told Dorothy. It had no electric lights, she said, and the facilities seemed a mile away from the bedrooms. It was boring and they preferred their other homes that had swimming pools and tennis courts.

We were standing by a huge yew tree and I pressed Alice to tell my wife the legend of Pernštejn. "Some time around the year 1000," she responded, "a wandering pilgrim came on workers hewing the rocks for the castle's foundations. 'You'll never build it,' he said, plunging his staff into the rocky soil. 'This staff will sooner bear leaves than your rocks will grow into a castle.' Surprisingly the staff sprouted green leaves and the castle was built.

"But there's more to the story. A hundred years ago, when my great-grandfather was living here, a great storm broke a branch off the old tree. Soon afterwards a balcony and battlement unexpectedly came tumbling down. Legend says that the castle will stand as long as the tree. So we'd better take good care of it!"

It took us more than an hour to make the rounds of the rooms and halls. The last was the "Hall of Conspiracy," dark and somber. It contained nothing but a great oval table and more than a dozen high leather-tooled chairs, each embossed with the coat of arms of one of the Moravian feudal families. This had been a secret room, its only entrance originally a hole in the ceiling. The windows had been constructed in differing sizes and at random, so that from the outside the existence of the hall was concealed. Here plots had been hatched, such as one in the early 17th century by the Moravian lords against the rebel families of the Bohemian kingdom. It had led to the Battle of the White Mountain in 1620, which marked the start of the Thirty Years' War.

Mani recounted all this to Dorothy, adding, "For you it's just a piece of European history, but for us who live here it's a tragic lesson, one I sadly fear we haven't learned. The truth is that these rich lands of Bohemia, Moravia and Silesia had a total population of three million; at the end of the Thirty Years' War there were only one million left.'' He walked over to a window; ''All those villages you see in the plains, including Křižanov and our castle, were burned to the ground. The Catholic Party under the Habsburgs had won a Pyrrhic victory.''

My wife was fascinated. ''What happened to Pernštejn?'' she asked.

''It stood impregnable, untouched,'' said Mani wryly. ''It was the poor peasant tenants down below who suffered.''

''Mani,'' said Alice, ''we'd better hurry if we're going to get to my brother's party on time . . . Oh no! Here comes Petrus. God save us! Now we'll never get away.''

The veteran warden of the castle was shocked that we hadn't visited several places, including ''the step of the Grey Lady.'' Nothing for it but to show Dorothy the imprint of the lady's foot in the solid rock floor, ''left five hundred years ago by that unhappy ancestor – before America existed, Gracious Lady!''

At last the old man, spouting ancient lore to the end, gently closed the door of our automobile, bowing as though it were a golden carriage, and we raced along bumpy roads to Rožínka. Until the end of the 18th century all this area, with its many villages, had belonged to the Rožínka estate. Then, during the 19th century many of the farms and villages had been freed and given to the peasants. After the end of World War I some of the larger farms which the family had retained were turned over to farmers during the land reforms. Our progress was slowed several times as Mani steered and honked his way through flocks of geese, ducks, chickens, sheep, goats – and half-naked children.

When I had phoned Alice's brother Vladimír, known to us all as Vlaschi, to propose our visit, he had insisted, ''Come tomorrow! Come for tea and tennis and stay if you can for stalking and dinner. Everyone is looking forward to meeting your bride!''

As we drove, Alice was now trying to sort out for Dorothy

all her relatives, most of whom still lived on neighboring estates. It was a congenial and to some extent an exclusive world. As Alice's flow of cousins, aunts and uncles and their balls, parties, shoots and hunts continued, I broke in to ask her if I might air the family skeleton for Dorothy.

"It went like this: Mama's grandmother, Countess Hardeck, inherited large estates and considerable wealth while still young. One day a young adventurer without title or money obtained service on her estates and rose to become manager. Finally she fell madly in love with him and against the family's wishes they were married."

This able young man, I continued, was my great-grandfather. He became an acknowledged authority on agriculture and reforestation and was knighted by Emperor Franz Joseph. It was said that one day Count Hardeck made a derogatory remark at Court about great-grandfather. On hearing about it the Emperor confronted Hardeck; "Dear Count," he said, "I only wish I had someone of von Teuber's caliber on every one of my crown lands." Despite this rebuke, the Hardecks, although cousins, issued instructions that no one in the family was to recognize great-grandmother's family. That disdain was carried on until Mama's generation.

Alice smiled: "What amazes me is the way your father has gone ahead through the years without letting such undercurrents touch him. He has everyone's respect and friendship."

I agreed and felt it was all the more surprising since Papa's family tree was new in comparison to Mama's and our neighbors'. Most could point to twenty or more generations of noble blood; Papa's had only three.

When Mani pulled up in front of Rožínka I watched Dot's eyes grow big as she scanned its bell tower, crowned with the onion-shaped cupola distinctive to this countryside, its Baroque facade and chapel. Rožínka was "small" by Moravian standards – a mere fifty rooms – but livable and charming. Lawns sloping down to the tennis court and swimming pool were dotted with groups of men and women chatting around tables under bright blue and white sun umbrellas. Liveried servants were deftly passing tea and sandwiches. The backdrop for an Oscar Wilde play, I said to myself, sleek, well-bred folk in understated, casual costume, product of Savile Row or a Viennese or Paris couturiere. (It was a closely guarded secret that there were a few village seamstresses who wielded able scissors.)

Above the scene floated snatches of bright, brittle conversation in modulated tones punctuated by the tinkle of laughter. I glanced at Dorothy, wondering if she was as cool as she looked. She must know she was the show piece on display.

Vlaschi advanced slowly to greet us, tall, dark and distinguished, with his long, heavily jowled face framed by deep sideburns. I caught his approving look as he covertly appraised my wife, kissed her hand and led her into the depths of the "voisinage" – cousins, aunts, uncles by the score. He was kidding them now – "See you all live up to Putze's description of us!" (Putze was my nickname among the young.) "You can be sure it was glowing rather than accurate, or she wouldn't be here!"

I had coached Dorothy on a piece of Austrian snobbery; she should address all women, regardless of age or relationship, by their first name and should use the familiar "Du", ignoring titles. All men who were related should be addressed the same way; with other men, young or old, she should use their titles and the formal "Sie". The inference was that "one ought to know who was who."

Dorothy suddenly gave me a sharp jab in the ribs, with a tense and audible whisper, as a guest approached, "Is he a 'Du' or a 'Sie'?" A friendly laugh went up around us. Her limited and American-accented German charmed, disarmed and entertained. Du's and Sie's were soon forgotten. The ice was broken. Dorothy seemed to be accepted.

As we made the rounds I was interested in some revealing remarks and questions. Lily, Countess Dubsky, Alice's second sister, cornered Dot. "I'm so interested in getting your views on what's going on in the world," she remarked. "What do you feel about Hitler?"

Her sister Maritschi broke in, "In our part of Moravia the German separatist movements are growing. I've just read a book by Rosenberg, the philosopher of the Nazi Party. He speaks about the superiority of our Aryan race; you know, the Germanic tribes. All very interesting, and I don't mind belonging to a superior race."

Lily asked, "What do you think, Dorothy, about race superiority? I don't see why anyone would want anything better than what we have here in Moravia. We get along perfectly well with the Czechs. They have always served us wonderfully. I don't see why we can't all keep getting along – Czechs, Slovaks, Austrians."

Someone else chimed in, "Don't you think Hitler is a bit ridiculous with his little Charlie Chaplin mustache and that long lock hanging down his forehead? But he seems to put a spell over people, women especially – what do you feel about him?"

Our procession of introductions was interrupted by a summons to prepare for our tennis match with Lily and her husband. We quickly changed our clothes and played a good hard game in which we were narrowly beaten; just as well, I thought, since Lily took her tennis so seriously. Afterwards we stretched out in the long wicker chairs, sipping strong coffee topped with cream.

I glanced up to see Uncle Carl Haugwitz joining us, together with his son Heinrich and Papa. Uncle Carl, really Alice's uncle, was a large muscular man with an open genial face, a country squire of the old Moravian school. His stately Schloss Námněšť was the closest castle to us, and Heinrich had been my closest friend. He had married a beautiful Hungarian countess.

"I'm glad you finally brought your bride to see us," Uncle Carl boomed. "Where are your Indian feathers, my dear?" he asked Dorothy. "And I see you don't have your husband wearing moccasins yet!" He broke into an open-throated laugh, then went on teasing her about things American. How did she like these Moravian castles? Not quite Spanish or Frank Lloyd Wright. "That fellow Wright rented your father-in-law's shootings during the Depression. Terrible shot – couldn't hit a pig in a barnyard."

Then he became serious. "But I'll wager those smaller new-fangled houses of yours are more practical these days, when we have to count our pennies. Our great conglomerations cost a fortune to run." I had heard from Papa that Uncle Carl ran his properties with painstaking care, despite his lavish entertainment of royalty and nobility. He was elaborating on the uncertain future for the great estates when our host Vlaschi strolled up.

"No more of your miserable predictions, Uncle Carl," he said. "I'm just back from Monte Carlo, Nice and Paris, and in those centers of gossip all the talk was about our emerging from the Depression and prosperity around the corner. I heard you talking about Hitler. That little man will soon be drowned in the wave of prosperity." He paused and laughed. "Or maybe he'll ride it to the top. After all, Germany needs its hero!"

Vlaschi went on to say that he himself was experiencing improved business conditions. He had sold his last large shipment of lumber on the international market for a much better price than any during the last five years. "And what's more," he added, "I believe I got a better price than your SVAZ could have obtained for me."

Vlaschi had the immediate attention of Papa and Uncle Carl. SVAZ was the Association of Large Land Owners, of which both were members of its powerful board of directors and for which both had worked hard to build up its operations and achieve higher prices on the international and domestic markets. I knew that Vlaschi had turned down membership in order to avoid the work involved. As the ladies drifted away from this man's conversation Papa and Uncle Carl began questioning Vlaschi about the identity of his dealer. He admitted he had used a large Jewish dealer in Prague.

"Those Jews are clever," he argued, "and they have their connections with others of their race abroad. My honored friends, you'll never beat them through SVAZ."

Papa looked angry, affronted not only in his loyalty to his organization but also in his anti-Semitic feelings. He spoke sternly to Vlaschi, "We landowners need to stand together. Had we done so after the war in the face of the government, when we were confronted with agrarian reform, we would have lost less land and less goodwill. We would have kept some of the execution of the law in our own hands and the country would have avoided a great deal of the corruption we have seen since."

Vlaschi shrugged and made no reply. He was not about to over-step the subtle boundary of respect and familiarity that regulated the generations of our noble families. Moreover, he recognized the regard in which Papa was held among his fellows.

I felt a temptation to voice some convictions, but decided now was not the time and place. Since I'd been away in America I had gained a new perspective on the forms and traditions that bound our aristocratic society together. "Honor" and "Honesty" were words emblazoned on our coats of arms, but I realized that they often became pragmatic tools to enhance the power and authority of us landowners to achieve our own ends at the expense of the government or other classes.

Others were now arriving for the dinner dance, some having driven from as far away as Germany, Hungary, and even Monte Carlo. After a lively dinner at which my wife was an entertaining novelty the dancing began. I watched to see how she would cope with the constant "cutting in" by one male after another. As she floated in green chiffon, her spirits as high as her color, the climax came when German Prince H. approached her to claim his turn at a Viennese waltz. Her enthusiastic performance matched his elegant step. When the waltz ended I went up to him, bowing with due propriety and said, "Highness, I think my wife has not been formally presented to you."

"Nein," proclaimed Dorothy, looking up at him, "Aber du tanze wie nie ein ander!" (No, but you dance like nobody else!) He looked amazed at her lack of formality, then roared with laughter and swept her away for another dance.

A couple of days later Papa asked Mani and me to join him at a meeting of the directors of SVAZ to be held in Brno – always Brunn to us. We drove in our large shiny Tatra, with our wives, Papa sitting erect, hands folded over the oak cane planted between his legs, Karmazín, our chauffeur, equally erect at the wheel, intense and morose. The words that passed occasionally between them were always to do with the Tatra.

I had known Karmazín ever since I was a young boy. He was the son of our fishmaster, who had lived on Sklenny Lake until one day his body was found floating in its water. Papa had assumed financial responsibility for the wife and two boys, who had played with Mani and me and studied with our tutor. Karmazín had learned German. As young boys we had been companionable up to that point that defined the difference of our two worlds. Our ways parted; Karmazín was promoted to chauffeur and I became Sir Doctor, young heir to Křižanov. I wondered now what went on behind those silent features.

This morning we drove through the prosperous agricultural plains, the fields and farms that had flourished under the Bohemian Crown. Two cultures had lived here, Slav and Germanic, their relations the key to prosperity. Whenever their religious or nationalistic differences had flared up, as they had from time to time, economic life declined. But at one time, when harmony reigned, Prague in the 14th and 15th centuries had become the center of European culture.

As we entered the outskirts of Brno Papa turned to Dorothy; "See that old mill? It once belonged to cousins of ours. Maria Jeritza used to work in it. A far cry from her singing at the Metropolitan!"

Around us now was a district of high walls and tall iron chimneys from which belched smoke. Old cranes clanked and coal-burning locomotives hauled products into the railroad yards. Behind small, soot-coated windows people labored in somber machine-filled rooms. Despite advanced social and labor laws the environment and working conditions were far from good. Some of the mills in this well-known textile city were Czech-owned, but the majority belonged to Germans and Jews.

Papa called Dorothy's attention to one of the largest and grimiest buildings once owned by his great-grandfather, at one time the largest spinning mill on the European continent. "Down the road there you can see the palace he built, at which he entertained sumptuously." Father's voice reflected the mixture of pride and disdain with which he regarded the origin of the Teuber share of our fortunes. He himself was at home only on the land.

The center of Brno was a dramatic contrast to the industrial suburbs. The spires of Gothic churches shared the skyline with Baroque palaces, now occupied by banks and insurance companies. This second-largest city of Czechoslovakia was proud of its long established opera and municipal theater. It had been the home of Mendel, Augustinian monk, founder of the science of genetics, as he tended his peas in the monastery garden.

We men dropped off the ladies in the shopping center and went on to SVAZ headquarters. The meeting was presided over by Count Alfi, a slow-moving and confident gentleman who brought the meeting to order quietly, with a cigar clamped between his lips. At his side was Prince Louis, among whose family were the largest landowners in Moravia. He himself was noted for the able administration of his estates and the care for his employees. Uncle Carl represented the German-speaking landowners of Southern Moravia.

Mani and I, as visitors, sat listening to the order of business which dealt largely with the legal and economic questions facing the association and some individual owners. Founded during the days of revolutionary ferment after the First World War, the association's main objective continued to be protecting the landowners from further expropriation of their land. Before 1919, when the agrarian reform began in newly independent Czechoslovakia, one thousand families on their large estates owned approximately 26 per cent of the total area of the country; some ten million acres were contained in two thousand large estates.

Now the land reform was in its final stages. Some five million acres had been expropriated from the original owners and distributed to small farmers in varying amounts, depending on the fertility of the land and other economic and social factors. The new government had taken into consideration areas where the need was greatest and land hunger the most urgent. The aims were high, but there had been flagrant abuses. Both nationalism and corruption had played their part. Predominantly Austrian and German landowners had had to cede more land on the excuse of "national security." As a result some Czech settlers were given land more readily than poor German-speaking peasants who were at least in as great need. This meeting of the association was still dealing with questions that had arisen out of all these complicated proceedings. What it did not address, I noted with some apprehension, were the larger economic and social needs of the country.

The session lasted several hours and as I walked outside I ran into Karmazín talking to what looked like another meeting, this one of chauffeurs. His voice was low, although his gestures were vehement. I couldn't hear what he was saying, but the tone of his voice sounded bitter. As soon as he saw me he stopped abruptly. I wondered what it was all about. It was not until several years later that I was shocked to learn its nature.

5

The Shoot

THE GREATEST EVENT of Papa's year was the partridge shoot in mid-September. It was a major happening in the lives of all the gentry. Shoots started with the woodcock, black-cock and grouse in early spring. Through the summer they shot roebuck and deer. In late September and early October it was the turn of the roaring stag. Finally, amidst the light snow of November came the shooting of hundreds of hare, rabbits and pheasants. The sporting year closed with formal balls in full ceremonial dress.

For weeks the foresters and gamekeepers had reported to Papa on the number of coveys of partridge maturing among the crops. By the second week of September the wheat, barley, rye and oats had been harvested and the covers for the birds were reduced to the fields of potatoes and beets.

The six days of shooting were planned as carefully as any battle campaign; shooting sites in the open fields were mapped so that waves of birds could be steered into posi-tion for the final drive, when the prowess of the seven or eight guns could be displayed. Each stand that was to be occupied by a guest was evaluated, the ones with the best opportunities being allotted to the most honored. Papa was by now an expert at this game. Mani and I, as the sons of the house, were of course allotted the ends of the line, the least promising stands.

As the day of the first shoot approached excitement spread from our household and gamekeepers and foresters to the villagers who would take part as beaters and carriers and the young boys who would be "picker-uppers" of the birds.

47

Each had his assigned role, like a football player. Each gun's strengths and weaknesses were discussed minutely. Even our house servants were involved in the uproar as they looked forward to the arrival of the valets and maids who accompanied the visiting gentry.

Papa had everything planned to perfection, down to the last detail; first came the hunting breakfast, then the noon meal served between drives in a shaded spot. Later in the day there would be a sumptuous tea, followed by dinner and dancing far into the night. Usually he planned the six partridge shoots in groups of three days, each a few days apart. A few privileged guests such as Count Carl Haugwitz, Alice's father Count Mittrowsky, and Prince Hansi Rutiborg came to all the shoots.

At exactly eight o'clock on the morning of this year's first shoot some of the best shots to be found anywhere in the world assembled around the large table to partake of Rosa's justly famous hunt breakfast – all manner of eggs, ham, sausages and those ravioli with *sauce piquante* to which most of the men looked forward. Along with Prince Hansi on Mama's right and Count Carl on her left, were Count Rudolf, with his inevitable early morning cigar, Count Louis and Count Vlaschi. As usual, Mani and I graced each end of the table.

Forty minutes later, Papa gave a gentle toot on his small silver hunting horn and all chatter stopped. His hunting dog began to whine and was sternly hushed. This was the anxiously awaited moment when stands were allocated. Papa gave each in turn his number and was formally thanked by each. Then waiting cars drove the party, including the ladies, who would discreetly accompany their men, to the shoot. There the foresters, splendidly arrayed in their dark green uniforms, took charge of the guests and conducted each to his stand. Papa, who refrained from shooting in order to give his whole attention to the proceedings, walked briskly to the center of the line, waited until each gun signalled that he was ready, then sounded his resonant, authoritative horn and the whole line began to advance.

For Papa this was a great moment and perhaps the last of its kind for a while; the Depression years, together with some catastrophic hoar frosts, had had their effect on the estate's finances and he had been forced to rent next year's shootings to foreign guns.

"Tire Haut!" (Shoot high!) cried a forester and his gentleman gun began firing at the whirring covey of partridge. In quick succession the others followed and small white cotton puffs arose in the morning air. As he led the line, Papa's grey eyes flashed right and left, making sure that all the participants obeyed the rules. Occasionally a gentleman was known to "make a sack," hold back from the shooting line in order to shoot overhead at birds flying back along the line. This practice was frowned on and Papa would shout angrily at the forester (never the guest) where the line was being held back. Only with a straight line could each guest be sure of his fair chance. And every gun was passionately determined to score high.

As gamekeepers and beaters moved to the next stands the gentlemen surrounded Papa. The tally of birds was completed and the lower scores assigned the better stands. "Please, gentlemen," admonished Papa, "keep the line straighter this time." The next drive was completed and the score tallied and then we moved on to the most celebrated part of the shoot. Below us stretched a long meadow and then higher ground covered with brush and wood cut low to make a thick cover. Around it were fields of potatoes and beets, ideal cover for the partridge. A gentle wind blew directly from the hillside, altogether a perfect setting.

The half-hour's wait for the beaters to work their way into position now gave me an opportunity for conversation with two men outside my social circle. With Dorothy beside me, I started talking with young Destilly, manager of our cooperative who was helping as a loader, and Tichý, the new teacher in our village school, who had been giving me lessons in Czech history and improving my speaking of the language. He had asked tentatively if he might walk along with me.

Tichý said he had read a recent article in a Moravian review in which I had been described as "the young scion of the estate owner of Křižanov who is said to have come back to his country seat with daring plans and humanitarian principles for democratic reform." (Fortunately the article had appeared in Czech and so had not come to Papa's attention.)

"What do you and Her Gracious Lady feel about the election of President Roosevelt?" asked Tichý. "He has just helped Russia have a chance to join the League of Nations – what does America feel about that?"

"We both believe firmly in his social reforms," I said. "They are unfortunately necessary. However, their effectiveness will depend on the willingness of people to accept the discipline of carrying them out. But, tell me, what do you men feel about the situation in this country?"

"If you mean how we stand as regards social reform," Tichý answered, with a snap of his fingers, "there's not much to be seen anywhere. I'm back recently from Slovakia. Ten years ago some of us young Czech teachers, doctors and others left home to help our Slovak brothers develop their schools and cultural life. What response did we get from them? Eternal gratitude? We got the sack! That's why I'm here. They say that we are taking jobs away from Slovaks. The very boys in whose wooden heads we sweated blood to knock something – those boys are now pushing us out. I tell you, there's a lot of feeling between us Czech and the Slovaks."

"But President Masaryk," I protested, "he's half Czech and half Moravian, isn't he helping to pull the country together?"

"He's a great man, but what can one man do?"

I started talking to these two young men about my ambivalent feelings towards the President. Like most of my fellow Austrians I had grown up resenting the break up of the Empire and hating the men who had architected the new country, Czechoslovakia, which had been carved from it – Masaryk, Beneš, Kramář and the rest. But during the past year I had read much of Masaryk's writings and had come to admire his thoughts about people, politics, philosophy and religion. More than that, I felt that he lived according to his beliefs.

"We Austrians," I told them, "talk a good deal about honor and patriotism, but I sometimes feel we should take a lesson from the President in thinking for the whole country and not just for our own class and culture."

I had to smile at the shocked surprise on the faces of the two men. Destilly blurted out, "Sir Doctor! You, the son of a landowner and a *Sudetiak* – excuse me – singing the praises of Tomáš Masaryk! Whatever would your father say?" (*Sudetiak* was the derisive name recently being given by Czechs to German-speaking citizens. It derived from the Sudetenland, the Czech territory bordering Germany, where most of the German-speakers lived.)

Destilly, obviously feeling he'd been too outspoken, was now looking embarrassed. I shook him playfully by the shoulder and he regained his poise. "What Tichý says about the Slovaks is true, but I talk to many of those who come here to work, and they feel that we Czechs act so superior to them. It's hardly a wonder that they're clamoring for autonomy and independence." He turned to Tichý: "I suppose they feel dominated by us the way we feel dominated by Austrians and Germans."

Destilly's feelings were mounting. He went on to talk about the eleven political parties among the Czechs and Slovaks, in addition to the German and Hungarian minority parties. With all that division, how could the country stand up to that man Hitler – or Stalin? His voice was rising and I could see gamekeeper Franz, my loader, stirring uneasily. I knew what he must be thinking – this kind of talk was not the kind that Papa would appreciate. I warned my young friends that we must talk more quietly.

Dorothy had not been able to follow our conversation and I now translated for her. She wanted to know from the Czechs how it was that so many Germans had settled in the country and why they had remained separate. In the United States, she said, most immigrant nationals had melded together.

Teacher Tichý was in his element as he outlined for my wife the history of German involvement in his country. It had begun, he said, a thousand years ago, when they were invited in by rulers as craftsmen, builders and teachers. As time went by religious and social dissensions arose, and a number of Czech kings called in German reinforcements to strengthen them against rival lords.

He turned to me, "You are right, Sir Doctor, about President Masaryk. He has stressed many times that Germans and Austrians are not second-class citizens. They were invited to be part of our nation with their full cultural rights."

"And on our side," I responded, "we Austrians haven't done our share of reconciling. We need to label our 'righteous indignation' as the hatred it really is."

Destilly chimed in; he was a socialist and concerned at the slowness of our social progress. There was so much corruption today in our government that younger men like himself had become very cynical. Part of the trouble was that President Masaryk was in his eighties and so frail and the men under him took advantage of him.

"Yes," I responded with a grin. "I wish he knew there was one of those *Sudetiaks* who appreciates what he's trying to do."

"Well, Sir Doctor," said Destilly, with a mischievous gleam in his eye, "don't you think that here is a good place to start making your feelings known?" He waved a hand along the line of guns. "These good lords maybe don't actually hate us Czechs, but they do look down on us. I feel it every day."

I admitted he was absolutely right. But couldn't we work together? Didn't the two of them feel that our crowd was a relic of the past and needed to be eliminated? And maybe we would be, unless we learned to live differently. But together, Czech, Austrian, Slovak, German – couldn't we demonstrate something that Europe and the world very much needed to learn?

Expressions of hope and incredulity flickered across those usually taciturn features. Whatever they might have replied was cut short by subdued cries around us. The hunt was on and we scrambled to our positions. For the next twenty minutes covey after covey flew over us and a thunderstorm of shots brought falling birds around us. Purdys, Holland-Hollands, Greeners and Browning automatics were all used with a speed and skill beautiful to watch. Each gentleman used two or three such guns and often as many loaders. Dorothy's appreciation of that skill was mixed with pity for the wounded partridge, for not everyone among us had the expertise to shoot "clean," so that the birds fell dead.

The cannonade over, dogs and boys with baskets were collecting the fallen birds and the gentlemen were making up their scores. To no one's surprise, the final score of all the birds found and the combined scores of all the guns did not exactly tally – 330 birds were spread out in rows on the meadow; the combined accounting of the hunters was 375. Prince Hansi topped the list with 91 birds. Like the rest of us he was flushed with excitement. There was much mutual congratulation, some carefully subdued bragging and not a little concealed jealousy. Still stimulated, the lords, their ladies and retinues followed Papa to the *Jagdfrühstück*, the hunt luncheon.

In a grove of pines, shafted with golden sunshine, stood a long table spread with fine linen and decked with the beautiful china and glassware for which Czechoslovakia was famed. Another table was more simply set for the foresters, loaders and village guests. Gamekeepers and beaters settled on the ground to munch their black bread and sausage.

Mama arrived with her three dogs, primly appearing at the shoot, which she tolerated in her resigned fashion. To each, according to rank, she extended her hand for the ritual kiss, from honored guests to villagers. We ate well and drank carefully of the beer, wine or *slivovic* as we kept the afternoon's business in mind. Then once again Papa's horn sounded and we strode to the next drive.

All went well until the last drive, when Prince Hansi calculated that he still needed a dozen more birds in order to reach the coveted total of 300 for the day. Mani, on the wing next to our honored guest, noticed that Hansi was lagging behind. Papa must have noticed also, because his message was passed along to move faster. As the coveys winged their way toward the line Hansi's "sack" became more pronounced. The whole line became disorganized. Oblivious, Hansi continued shooting feverishly.

The final formalities ended the day's hunt. Thirteen hundred partridge and quail were laid out in rows. To one side the guns were comparing scores. The head forester now stepped forward, removed his hat and intoned, "Hunter's hail! Your Graces. Obediently I beg to announce the bag of today's hunt: 1,326 partridge, 47 quail, 5 ducks, 1 hawk and 3 various game."

"Hunter's hail!" we all replied.

A chorus of "Wonderful!" "Excellent!" from the guests.

"Yes, gentlemen, my foresters and gamekeepers, the hunt went well," declaimed Papa. Then a stern note entered his voice; "But what in heaven's name went wrong on your wing, Forester Nederly, on the last drive? I cannot understand, Mani, why you on the far wing were so far ahead and disrupted the line? I was ashamed to see a great day of shooting so spoiled. I have told you again and again . . ." Papa's scathing reprimands mounted. He had sufficient sense of justice not to let the blame fall on his forester, but he picked on Mani to get at Hansi, the culprit, who was standing nonchalantly nearby, smug and unconcerned.

Mani grew redder and redder and finally burst out,

"Forgive me, Papa, but you know perfectly well that this was neither my fault, nor the fault of Forester Nederly. I don't want to be impolite , but I think the person responsible for the sack knows exactly what I'm talking about."

"Let us go into this no further," Papa answered sternly. "I will not have my shoots ruined and you, my son, must be responsible."

At this point my old rebellious spirit rose beyond control. "Why should Mani or anyone take the blame," I spat out bitterly, "for what you did, Hansi? You know you made the sack — just for a few birds. It's disgusting!"

Papa looked incredulous and then deeply pained. He turned on his heel and walked away to the waiting cars. He left behind total silence, and then slowly the company followed him. I sensed silent approval from the foresters and gamekeepers. But as Dorothy and I made our way to our room to change for dinner I began to feel ashamed of myself. My outburst had been fueled by more than my anger at Hansi and Papa. There was an element of social indignation there. I argued with myself and then with Dorothy, but finally admitted that Papa's and Hansi's wrongs did not justify mine. I must apologize for my rudeness.

Papa was the hardest to approach and I drew him aside first, told him I was deeply sorry and asked him to forgive me for my infernal pride. He had tears in his eyes. "That you, my son, should insult one of our honored guests in public! Are you apologizing in principle, or do you really mean it?" I told him I was truly sorry.

Hansi was easier. He waved away my apology with a smile. Then I spoke in front of all the rest so that Hansi might be publicly cleared. Relief was apparent on all the faces; the gentleman's code of honor and courtesy had been restored. The resplendent hunt dinner was back on track; Papa and Mama cirulated among their guests, gathered around the shining white stoves and the huge open fireplace in the great drawing-room. The butler and his footmen deftly passed hors-d'oeuvres and glasses of sparkling wine.

Everyone was present except Hansi. I saw Papa glance at his watch and I could guess his feelings; no guest should ever hold up a perfect dinner for a moment. Suddenly the salon doors opened wide and on the threshold stood Hansi, his shirt front gleaming white, emerald studs glowing. His ruddy face was lit up with a wide, innocent smile. In his hand he held a single, long-stemmed red rosebud.

For a moment he stood there, all eyes focussed on him; in silence he walked across the room to where Mani, Alice, Dorothy and I were standing. With a gallant, low bow he presented the flower to Alice. It was Hansi's elegant form of apology.

6

The Decision

DOROTHY AND I arrived at the breakfast table the following Sunday to find Papa and Mama had already begun to eat. They welcomed us to the table.

"Thanks, Papa. Dorothy will take a cup of coffee; I'll have breakfast later as I'd like to go to Communion."

Papa frowned. "That's too bad; it's all ready for you." He stared at me severely. "We are all attending High Mass in our chapel. It will be an important occasion. The Mayor and leading citizens will be there. Shouldn't you be dressed a little more formally?"

I felt like a boy again, as I had stood before him so many times dressed in my stiff collar, tight jacket and bowler hat clamped on my head. His disapproval had always made me sulk, but now I managed to grin and agree to run up and change. Here we go again, I thought. Papa had obviously staged this ceremonial Mass as an occasion at which he, as "Patronus," would display his heir with his bride to the ranking citizens of his domain. It was only incidentally a religious observation.

Dorothy and I followed Papa and Mama solemnly through the castle portals and down the slope to where many of our employees and their wives were assembled. They greeted my parents submissively, kissing their hands, then turned to welcome Dorothy and me, eager to glimpse the bride. Then they fell in line behind us to march up Chapel Hill. At the church door the village and estate dignitaries were lined up – mayor, police chief, school principal, our manager, director and foresters. As we made our entrance into the chapel the organist broke into the "Te Deum" and our family took our places on the cushioned benches along the walls of the apse next to the altar.

Dorothy was wide-eyed as she stared around at the five hundred-year-old stone walls and high ceiling, graced by a great Venetian glass chandelier on which the light of a hundred candles flickered, more candles on the main and side altars framing a picture of Saint Barbara, patron saint of the chapel. The pulpit, richly painted in wine, blue and gold, stood out dramatically against the heavy dark walls.

Now came the Father, preceded by candle-carrying servers and followed by his deacons, bowing in unison to Papa, then to his family. The Mass unfolded in all its beauty and dignity, although conducted as always with great speed by our priest, and without a sermon – to Papa's satisfaction. As I glanced at Father F., I decided he had put on weight, not surprising in view of the frequent feasts with which he celebrated any possible event. It was always a banquet featuring the fatted pig, our national creature, served with sauerkraut, dumplings, cakes, wines and beer and crowned by the Czech liquor *slivovic* and the long thin cheroots.

My mind wandered from the service as I looked across at Papa, bent forward, not kneeling, with hands clasping the gnarled head of his oak walking stick. Papa, with firm belief in the sanctity of honor and tradition, family reputation and the perfection of his products. He looked self-sufficient, no apparent need for him of the Deity.

Mama, on the other hand, wore a troubled look. She wants so much out of life, I thought, fighting obstacles and hardships that are so often of her own creation, and in spite of her great talents, resenting and resisting God.

Mani and Alice were next to us. My mind went back to the Jesuit school where Mani and I had forged a common bond of faith and friendship. I felt sad that he and Alice seemed so insecure, despite all their material well-being. My attention strayed to the dignitaries, some of them whispering and smiling together, oblivious of the service; the steady chant of devout women from the back benches and their menfolk standing behind them, sometimes slipping out for a quick smoke. Not a very devoted congregation, I thought – then suddenly realized the humor of the situation, my judging others while my own mind was wandering.

I began to feel ashamed of myself, so often critical of my family and these good neighbors. I had rebelled against Papa's conservative authority and what I felt was the out-of-date social order he was trying to maintain. I had blithely taken off for a brighter, more promising world – democratic, free and liberal America, leaving behind my country, with all its confusion and confrontations. In the new world I had gone my pleasure-loving way.

This was not the first time I had felt guilt about my easygoing years. Back in San Francisco I had been moved by a compulsion to return home, not just to have Dorothy received into the family, but also to make amends in some way for my profligate years.

But back now at home, I had been frustrated by doubts as to what I could do that would be relevant to the situation in my community and homeland. It was one thing to play my part as a responsible son and neighbor. But what could I do realistically as a citizen of Czechoslovakia, a land still plagued by its original diversities and divisions?

As I knelt in that chapel an altogether unexpected thought entered my mind. The conviction was born in my spirit that I should seek out the first citizen of the country, Tomáš Masaryk, and as an Austrian with all candor ask his forgiveness for my attitude towards the Czechs. At once my pride resisted the idea. You will look foolish. And what can just one of your class, race and breed accomplish? There are others, older and wiser than you who would carry more weight. And anyway, it's too late for such a gesture.

And yet, a voice inside me said I must do it. When Communion was celebrated I went up to the altar rail with Mani and Alice and there sealed my resolve to bear my responsibilities for my native land, Czechoslovakia, as well as for my adopted home, America.

Mass over, I led Dorothy over to meet the priest and took the opportunity to tell him how much the Mass had meant to me and of my decision. He looked more than a little puzzled. "I am glad to meet Your Gracious Lady," he said, "and I am glad she is studying Catholic truth. If only people came to church more and listened to these truths, all would be well."

He looked at me seriously. "Certainly, our President is a great man. He is sincere, but he allows too much revolutionary ferment to grow. And there are others in the government who are no good. Now, why does the President favor this new nationalist church, an offshoot of the Hussites? They claim to have one and a half million members – perfectly absurd! Personally, I don't think we need all this so-called change, young Sir!"

The Father was now talking to me as he had done when I was his pupil and he went on to dispose of any need for change in the country. He was in truth yearning for the old days of the Austrian empire as he reminisced, enumerating the bishops and counts who had visited our estate and were related to our family. He talked about one of them, Count Hyun, both a count and a bishop.

I responded, "Yes, we all had to be on our best behavior, including Mama. She would sometimes forget to remain standing until His Excellency said grace before the meal and would plump herself down, revealing our unchristian ways for all to see!"

The pale, timid assistant pastor had joined us. He chimed in with his memory of the Bishop; he was fresh out of seminary and in a run-down parish when Bishop Hyun made his pastoral visit. The Bishop had walked into the church in his full majesty to inspect it, and there, leaning against the altar was a broom, left by an old absent-minded sexton. The Bishop grabbed the broom and chased the priests out of the church! Next morning he preached an acid sermon about those who neglected their duties, worse than heretics or Protestants!

Outside the church Dorothy and I made our way through the many groups, heading first to the gamekeepers in their grey and green hunting suits, hats studded with insignia, then to the foresters and on to the men and women employed in minor jobs on the estates. They were typical of Moravia, stocky, dour men and women, many showing the imprint in their limbs and faces of the heavy field work day after day. The women wore dark printed kerchiefs, fitted bodices and heavy, many-folded, long dark skirts; the men, rough dark suits, sturdy boots and caps or hats.

A group of younger men, gardeners, chauffeurs, school teachers, were more at ease with us; they wanted to know about life in America. I told them about my own varied experiences, working at the time of the Depression, including washing cars and selling baby carriages at Macy's. This they found very amusing, but scarcely credible. We moved on to politics. It seemed that they had a high regard for the American system of government.

"It was your President Wilson who helped our President set up our system after your model," said the young head gardener.

Our chauffeur, Karmazín, probably the most intelligent of these men, broke in at one point, objecting to a remark of mine about the importance of individuals taking responsibility for changing what they saw wrong around them. "Do you really think, Sir Doctor, that we can do away with the injustices and selfishness of people without changing the system of government everywhere – even in America?"

Papa's insistence that we greet the mayor prevented my response. Dorothy and I went the rounds of the *Honoratiores* (dignitaries) until my mouth was left dry with all the small talk and Dorothy's hand was limp with the kisses. When the last respects were said we turned in relief and walked back up the broad walk. Father was waiting for us, smiling; "You two should have greeted the *Honoratiores* first. But you did well, otherwise.'' High praise from Papa.

''Breakfast at last!'' cried Mani, heading Alice, my wife and me towards the kitchen. There it was, just as I remembered it, on the top floor of the brewery building, located so that none of its smells could waft into our living quarters. It was Rosa's domain, staffed by three women assistants and three men-servants. I looked longingly at the huge pots pushed to the back of the stove, recalling my craving for our youthful snacks of dark country bread, crisp rolls and warm milk with which Rosa used to regale Mani and me. No more! Our breakfast trays were formally lined up to be carried out to the terrace. First, however, Dorothy insisted on examining the kitchen. She looked with awe at the expanse of white tile floors and walls, in the center of the room the immense ten-burner stove, with its baking furnaces, and the larder and cold storage rooms.

The four of us sank gratefully into chairs around our belated breakfast on the terrace. ''Quite a morning,'' said my wife. ''But I hand it to Papa for carrying out such an occasion with style.''

''I suppose that's true,'' said Mani, ''but I must tell you that what really surprised me this morning was the way your husband reacted so pleasantly to Papa and everything. I was amazed when Genus meekly ran up to change his clothes. He's always turned sulky or muttered back to Papa and fidgeted all through Mass and looked so bored at meeting dignitaries.''

Mani peered at me and said quietly, ''Genus, you're different from the way you used to be.''

Alice said, ''Why, of course, he's become very American. I've noticed it, too. He's developed that democratic way of talking with everybody in a friendly way as though there were no class distinctions anymore.''

I was nettled by the suggestion that I was very American. ''The trouble is, the whole world is changing, but back here you don't recognize it.''

Mani shot back, ''You are right about things changing,

but why should we meekly accept changes when they threaten to sweep away everything that was stable? It sounds fine when that idealistic old President of ours destroys with the stroke of a pen some part of the old order, but does he ever know what happens when he draws a line through a village, even a backyard, and labels one half Czech and the other half Austrian?''

Mani went on agitatedly: Did Masaryk think you could change the furniture of a man's mind by law? Could you free a man of his cherished pride of race and heritage by decree? And if you took away part of his land, land his family had tilled for generations, in the name of reform, because someone else had less than he had — how could this new order win his allegiance?

It was my turn to be startled. Mani, mildest of men, was seldom vehement, except when we were young and I had deliberately provoked him. I said, "And yet, Mani, it's you who fight Papa and Mama for better living quarters for our people and better wages for someone who's underpaid. It's you who resent migratory Slovaks being herded on to our lands under conditions fit only for our cattle."

Mani looked a little sheepish. "I'm no reformer. It's just that I get a little tired of people like our President making speeches about democracy, when I see so little of it in every-day life. The politicians seem to think you can cure the evils of society by a Treaty of Versailles. That's nonsense. Racial hatreds are too deep rooted.''

I replied that I had no intention of defending the Versailles Treaty, but we must face our Austrian part in making it necessary. We were young at the time of the last war, I reminded Mani; all it had meant to us was cold school corridors and ice in our wash pitchers; never enough to eat; Mama looking after the wounded in the castle hospital. So we weren't aware of how much of that war was our respon-sibility as Austrians. We had denied our own ability to give mature leadership. We had robbed this new nation of our support and cooperation.

Mani was wearing that stubborn look he always assumed when he wasn't sure of himself. Finally he shot back, "I find your definition of us Austrians a bit cruel, Genus. And that's a quality not entirely lacking among Czechs."

"Agreed. What you are saying is that Czechs and Austrians are not that different." I laughed. "Oh, I know you are thinking, 'Trite, unworthy of his Jesuit trained mind.' But the fact is, Mani, I see that my irresponsible, superior, devil-may-care Austrian attitude has harmed our Czechoslovakia, and I want to do something about it."

Alice chimed in with an impatient note, "So, Gene, what do you propose to do?"

To my own surprise I blurted out the conviction that had come to me at Mass: "I'm going to call on President Masaryk and apologize to him for my unhelpful attitude."

There was a long silence, then, "God Almighty!" from Mani. "What ever for? And what do you think Papa will say to that?"

I thought about it. "I really don't know. You might expect him to hit the roof. On the other hand, he understands how I think about the status quo and the need to launch out with new ideas — even though he may not approve."

"But, Gene, this is more than one of your 'parlor pink' ideas you used to play around with, isn't it?" asked Mani. "I say again that something basic seems to have happened to you since you've been in America. What is it?"

I felt squeezed into a corner. "Very well, it's true," I admitted. "The best way I can put it is that I'm finding a new orientation for my life."

I went on to tell Mani, as he already well knew, how over the years I'd always been intrigued with ideas about the meaning and purpose of life. My Jesuit training, no doubt! Well, one evening in San Francisco Dorothy's parents had taken us to a meeting that was different from any I'd ever been to. We listened to men and women, young and old, some of them from distinguished backgrounds, some college students, and from a number of countries. The theme of their remarks was that the world stood in great need of change (no argument about that in the midst of the Depression!) but that the necessary political, economic and social changes must be based on changes in individual attitude and behavior. Nothing very novel about that, but here was the catch. We Christians, they said, who talked about the need to bring back morality into the market place and the legislature, must ourselves live by the absolute standards of the Sermon on the Mount. Otherwise, we were still part of the moral compromises we criticized in society.

Mani replied thoughtfully that was all very well, but weren't these people a bit on the idealistic side? All through history mankind had pushed God's truth aside in trying to settle its differences. Man labeled his selfish goals "just causes" and "holy wars." I was only repeating the unrealities the Jesuits had talked to me about.

"The trouble was," I told him, "that I often had the feeling that my Jesuit friends didn't really expect me to apply their principles. And I didn't!"

"So, what's new this time?" asked Alice a little impatiently.

"Well, these people, some of whom I met later individually, didn't try to convince me about principles with which I was already familiar. Instead, they talked about making experiments, testing in my everyday life whether ideas worked."

"What ideas?" asked Alice.

First, I told her, the one I'd spoken about. Judging my motives and actions against absolute, instead of relative standards. And then they stressed something I was very familiar with through Father Ignatio's Jesuit training – being quiet and seeking God's direction. Only, these new friends had been even more practical, to the point of writing down the thoughts that came to me and being prepared to act on them. That was what had precipitated a big decision for me. I had soon discovered that I did not have the determination or courage to obey the directions that entered my mind, especially putting right wrongs I had done, without making a commitment to put my whole life into God's hands.

Alice sounded uncomfortable; "Aren't you just talking about obeying your conscience?"

"Yes, that is at the heart of it. Easy for a guy like me to say, hard to do!"

Dorothy spoke up. "Gene and I embarked on the same road and started by being truly honest with each other. It's made all the difference in our marriage! Nothing to hide, no need to pretend."

"Who are these saintly characters who made such a difference to you?" asked Mani.

I laughed. "They are no more saintly than you and me. They certainly aren't pious. They're just realistic about themselves and the world. I suppose the one truly distinctive thing about them is that they are one-hundred-per-cent committed."

"What do they call themselves?"

"They've become known as the Oxford Group, since a group of them who were students from Oxford were traveling together and were labeled that way by the press."

Alice took us back to the starting point of this conversation; "So, what are you going to say to President Masaryk?"

"Mani, that's where I'd very much appreciate your help. It's one thing to apologize for my arrogance as an Austrian, but you know so much better than I do what are the basic problems of this country, and what kind of assistance I could offer."

Mani seemed touched. "I expect you'll need help. I don't think I'd like to be in your shoes!"

I grinned: "Facing President Masaryk will be child's play compared to facing Papa!"

Schloss Křižanov c1930

Interior of Castle; Salon

Family Dining Room

Baron Eugene von Teuber (Papa) c1933

Countess Anna von Teuber (Mama) c1932

Gene von Teuber (author) c1932

Mani and Alice von Teuber (Gene's brother and sister-in-law)

The Shoot in full swing

The results of the Shoot at day's end

7

Confrontation

I HAD SUMMONED UP my courage and written to President Masaryk to ask for an appointment to meet with him. I sent it in a covering letter to his son Jan, whom I had met in London, when he was serving as ambassador. Very soon I received two replies, an informal one from the son and an official letter from the Office of the President of the Republic. Jan Masaryk had invited Dorothy and me to the summer residence of the President, where the whole family was staying. Jan wrote that his father was ill and might not be able to see us, but please come to lunch anyway.

Now the moment had arrived to break the news to Papa and Mama. Dorothy and I were sitting with them after breakfast. I produced the letters, which were written in English, and translated them for my parents. Papa reached for the letters, with their official seals, and stared at them in consternation. Then he burst out, "How can you run after this man and his family? They and their like did everything in their power to destroy our Austrian monarchy."

There was a long silence as he held the letters at arm's length as though they offended his nostrils. "Genus, you actually asked to see him?"

I nodded and Papa rose and began to pace before the fireplace as he did when his mind was in turmoil. "I should hate that old man! I *do* hate that Beneš and all his crowd who smashed our beloved empire." Papa sounded as though he was talking more to himself than to us. "And yet, when I hear the old President is gravely ill I tremble for the future."

Mama's voice rose angrily, "That whole bunch is no good

and Beneš is the worst of them. He wants to destroy everything we hold dear. All that talk of democracy – why, they are trying to deny us every privilege, everything that makes life worth living."

"I agree with you about Beneš," Papa said quietly, "but there's something about the old man in the Hradshin (the official palace) that makes it hard to hate him." He turned to me, "I've seen him just twice as part of a delegation of our SVAZ. They were official calls on him to make our just rights known. They weren't easy visits."

Papa went on to describe how the landowners fought determinedly and how Masaryk was just as determined. But the four conservative estate men had left the interview with respect for the President's sincerity, almost against their will. Papa added, however, that some of the land-owners, including his closest friend Vladimír, Alice's father, a normally kind and just nobleman, had consistently refused to meet Masaryk.

"I feel just as deeply as they do," Papa continued, "yet I have to admit there's a quality in the man without which we Austrians and Germans would have fared much worse than we have. It's strange; here he is, the son of an illiterate coachman of the Imperial House, yet himself a gentleman in the real sense of the word."

I could see Papa was in one of those moods when his basic integrity was wrestling with his prejudices. He broke off his pacing again and swung around on me; "Tell me, son, wherever did you get this idea of calling on him? And even worse, mixing with that family socially? I do not approve of it!"

Mama chimed in vehemently. "I fully agree with you, Eugene. I've noticed, Genus, that since your return you've tended to be familiar with all kinds of people. Where is your pride? And now these Masaryks, who've robbed us of land, privileges and even titles – why, this letter from the President's Office is addressed to plain 'Mr. Teuber'! Well, I can tell you, I'm not just 'Mrs. Teuber'! What has got into you, Genus?"

My pulse was racing. This was my chance to open my heart and my thinking to my parents as never before. I looked at them across the table, Mama so graceful, her face alive with her emotions, and Papa so dignified and disciplined, his integrity only limited by his understanding. How inexpressibly dear they were to me, and yet barbed barriers seemed to have sprung up between us. I prayed for the words I needed to reach across to them.

"A year or so ago I felt much as you both do. Your upbringing had taught me to honor, love and serve God, Emperor and country. Then that whole precious structure crumbled after the war. I, who had always been part of the ruling class, felt humiliated and ashamed. I'd come to think that we Austrians were vastly superior to the Czechs culturally and socially. You remember how we automatically thought of them as a nation of servants – excellent servants, of course, but there to serve us. Remember how the Viennese theaters and cabarets made fun of 'the dumb Czech', with a touch of condescending warmth? I felt so justified in my superiority and that fed my bitterness at becoming the underdog."

"Then how can you . . ." Mama began, but was waved into silence by Papa. He waited for me to continue.

The world was like a merry-go-round, I said. Races, countries, leaders, up one time, down the next. But the same hatreds, superiorities, greeds, fears and frustrations were going round and round and up and down in each rider. That was the history of our country. First the Czechs were riding high, then the Austrians came bounding up and the Czechs were down. Now it was the turn of the Czechs again. And they were making the same mistakes with us as we had made for centuries with them! Somehow there must be born in us that personal integrity which would bring people and nations to live together. All I could do was begin with myself.

"Noble sentiments," said Papa dryly. "I was under the illusion that I sent you to the best Jesuit school in Austria to learn such principles."

"If you hadn't, Papa, I might never have understood the

dilemma we face today, nor how far I'd strayed from the best I knew. I talked one way and lived quite another. I was so wrapped up in the blithe, intellectual, comfort-loving ways of a young Austrian, I'd become an ineffective, purposeless Christian."

Papa began pacing again. I could read what he was thinking – this kind of talk was only suitable for church, where he could close his ears when it invaded his personal privacy. "You've strayed a long way from the point of a visit to Masaryk."

"I only know that the President is deeply concerned about the growing divisions and the political corruption in the country. What we have to say may mean something to him."

Mama bounced up in her chair. "Do I understand you aright, Genus? Are you actually going to apologize to that lot? Apologize for what? It's time they apologized to us!

"I love our Moravian people," she went on. "They are still loyal. They like to work for me and they and I get along very well together. But that upstart pseudo-intellectual crowd who are running things in Prague are ruining everything with their talk of socialism, taxes and land reform. They should apologize for robbing us!"

I approached Mama on her blind side: "Did you know that Masaryk has had art historians and expert decorators repairing and redecorating the royal castle in Prague?" I told her about an excellent book by Karl Čapek I'd just read. He wrote that Masaryk said it would be a mistake to overlook the adherents of the monarchic regime. I said I agreed with him that democracy didn't exclude a useful and co-operative aristocracy. I believed it needed our help. And I added that Mama, with her taste, and Papa with his experience in economics and agriculture – why shouldn't we all help in building the right democracy?

Mama grew more restrained, but went on arguing that it was wrong that an inferior people should dictate to a more cultured and developed people. That was a point that Herr Hitler was making. She didn't agree with his methods but we must admit that through Henlein and his Sudeten-German front our people were finding some backbone again to assert our rights.

Papa, pursuing his own train of thought, maintained that whatever Masaryk's intentions might have been, the German sections of Bohemia and Moravia had suffered the most during the years of the Depression. There had been obvious favoring of Czech over German industries. He added, ''You were away in America during those years and probably didn't read anything there about these injustices. But don't you notice the tensions are much greater than when you were here last?''

I had to admit that I did, and Papa pressed on with his argument. It was all very well, he said, for Masaryk to have pushed through legislation intended to create ''a kind of Switzerland,'' to secure the rights of all national and cultural groups. But he had not managed to handle the men in his government who had succeeded in applying their vengeful attitudes to their former masters, the Austrian and Hungarian minorities.

Truly wound up now, Papa declared I should remember enough of my history to know that that situation went back to the time in 1918, when Clemenceau, the old French tiger at the Versailles Treaty Conference, had gone beyond Masaryk's demands in slicing out German, Hungarian and Austrian territories and incorporating them in the new state of Czechoslovakia. He had made a mockery of President Wilson's Fourteen Points and laid the foundations on which Eduard Beneš and his colleagues had built the national hatreds in their country.

''These are the facts, Genus, that you should lay before Masaryk — if you insist on seeing him. But I must make it clear to you that I still do not approve of such a visit.''

''Papa, I don't deny the facts. What I'm searching for is a solution to them.''

''Nevertheless,'' said Papa grimly, ''I consider such a visit undignified. You will also find it unprofitable and I want no part in it!'' He rose and left the room.

That morning school teacher Tichý arrived to give me my weekly lesson in Czech grammar and history. My degrees in Economics and Agriculture and my Doctorate of Law had all been in German, and as soon as I'd arrived home this time I decided I must become fluent in Czech in order to manage the estates efficiently when that day came. Recently I'd felt I must also be at home in the language so that I could play my part responsibly as a citizen. The session with Tichý was always stimulating since we ranged over human and political issues.

This morning Tichý proposed that we study the small world of our village; he said that if I really understood the complex life of Křižanov I would have a better grasp of the political and economic life of the country as a whole. With my visit with the Masaryks uppermost in my mind, that suited me just fine.

Křižanov had a population of about 1500, said Tichý, and was the largest village in a ten mile radius and a market center for a score of smaller communities. It had a school which went to the third grade of junior high and served the whole area and a church with three priests who did the same. Our modernized fire department, pride of the village, was poised at all hours of the day and night to deal with fires in the area; it had recently replaced a team of our estate horses and hand-pump with a motor.

The fire chief, Tichý continued, was the most socially prominent of the village ''official class'' — mayor, postmaster, priests, teachers and the like. It soon became apparent, however, that Tichý was very unhappy about the inferior status of the teachers. ''We are given the best education in Prague,'' he said, ''and Bohemia is the most cultured province in the country, but these Moravians are always trying to upstage us.'' The estate foresters, for example, wouldn't play cards with the teachers, and even Father F., the most popular priest, who came to Kilík's Inn for his couple of jugs of beer, never sat with the ''socialist'' teachers. And as for Hruby, the Communist leader in the village, on his rare visits to the Inn he always had to sit by himself.

"By the way," ventured Tichý, "Hrubý is said to be having an affair with Lushka, a young woman who works on your estate, so you can be sure that he knows just about everything that goes on in the castle."

Another purveyor of community gossip was old Mrs. Schmetz, who with her husband ran the general store. They spoke a mixture of German and Yiddish with broken Czech. Dr. Steinovský, the local medic, on the other hand, had only the slightest touch of Jewish accent. He had won the hearts of all by his kindness. He would never admit that the rising wave of anti-Semitism could engulf the country.

Tichý led me into the intricacies of local politics. Innkeeper Kilík was also the present mayor and owed his position to a coalition of the Agrarian and Peoples' Parties and a few National Democrats. My teacher said he was hoping that his own party, the Socialists, made up of artisans, small land holders and farm workers, would unseat the mayor at the next election, aided by the National Socialists. No one knew which way the Communists would go.

Last night, according to Tichý, the inn had been the scene of a hot debate that nearly came to blows. None of the parties could agree on a program for street improvement and water supply, and the City Council members had departed in disgust. It was ironic, said Tichý, that the five parties who had been fighting each other were the same ones who formed the government coalition under Prime Minister Malypetr in Prague. All over the country, it seemed, the same pattern of conflict and stagnations was holding up political progress and reform.

"And at least in this area we are all Czechs — apart of course from your own family. Can you imagine what it's like in the Czech-German border areas and in Slovakia, where there's racial diversity? We all give allegiance to the President, but we seem to be more divided as time goes by. Sir Doctor, you come from America. Those of us who have relatives over there hear from them that everything is marvellous, people are so rich and free. What is their secret?''

I told him that Czechoslovakia couldn't just copy the United States, nor Switzerland. Americans had to solve their own problems, and so did we. ''We have to build our own brand of democracy. President Masaryk has already set high standards of justice and unity and I believe they are attainable. We just need to get together and support him.''

My teacher's expression brightened. ''Yes, you are right, Sir Doctor. Our President has laid out the road.'' He shuffled in his briefcase and brought out a book. ''Here is one of his most recent statements. You read it please, and I'll check your accent.''

He handed me *Conversations with Karel Čapek* and pointed out a paragraph. I read Masaryk's words:

The longer I live the more I recognize the special part which the individual has in the development of mankind . . . . Higher endowment and what is often called 'luck' does not justify the exploitation of those less highly endowed and less lucky . . . . Revolution and dictatorship may sometimes be able to destroy what is bad but they do not create what is good and lasting . . . . Ethics I base on love, sympathy and humanity . . . . I can say from my own experience that for states and nations and for their administrators there is no other morality, no other ethical order, than there is for the individual.

''It's like holy writ to me,'' said Tichý. Then the light went out of his face. ''But our President is old now, and ill. He can't fight much more. Then what'll happen to us?''

''I suppose there's no easy answer,'' I replied. ''But if enough of us take this philosophy seriously and put these truths of his into practice with as much passion as he has, then his dreams could become reality.''

Two mornings later, Dorothy and I set off on our journey to visit the President. Jan Masaryk had offered to send a car to the Excelsior Hotel in Prague to pick us up. When we arrived there we found a note from him to say that the presidential car would arrive for us at 3:30 "to bring you to us at Castle Lány where at present the whole 'fam-damily' is happily assembled. All of us, including probably Father, will be delighted to see you."

As we waited in the hotel my mind went back to my last meeting with Jan Masaryk. Dorothy and I had spent an evening with him in London at the home of a relative of mine, the Honorable Enie Dudley Ward, one of London's liveliest hostesses. Jan in the eyes of the world was a shrewd and polished diplomat; in fact he was at that time an unhappy and insecure man. His marriage was about to break up and he was worried about his father's health and about his country's future. As we sat with him in a quiet corner of Enie's drawing room he had made it clear to us that London's brittle social life was palling on him.

The hotel porter announced the arrival of the car and we were on our way. It was a warm afternoon and as we left the outskirts of Prague we drove through fields being harvested by throngs of peasants. These Bohemian plains were richer than our Moravian highlands. I admired their sugar beets and an occasional vineyard. As we approached Castle Lány it was a relief to plunge into the cool of shady lanes.

Dorothy had been peppering me with questions about the Masaryk family and whom we might meet. I told her that in addition to Jan there would certainly be his sister Alice, who was in charge of the household. Dr. Alice was the President of the Czechoslovakian Red Cross and known as a formidable lady. Her younger sister, Olga Revilliod, married to a Swiss doctor, was perhaps the closest to their father.

Dorothy asked if there were likely to be others beside the family. I passed the question on to the chauffeur. He replied, "These days very few are allowed to visit, so I believe you will find only the family. When the 'Old Gentleman' was well people came in from everywhere, but now Dr. Alice is very strict." He added, "You must have something very special for him, Sir, to be here!"

We drove through the park gates and drew up at the entrance. The castle had once belonged to Prince Furstenburg, one of his smaller properties, and had been expropriated by the government to serve as the President's summer residence, close enough to Prague. Jan came through the entrance, gave us a heart-warming greeting and ushered us around the house to the garden terrace and introduced us to his two sisters.

"Hope you won't be bored with us," said Jan cheerfully, "no one but the family here. I'm sorry Father can't come down to see you, but possibly you and I, Gene, might go to his room after tea."

The memory of that tea-time is still bright in my mind. Madame Olga, gentle and calm, presiding over the tea table, Dr. Alice, dignified and a trifle forbidding, Jan talkative and restless. After a brief time of chit-chat I decided to plunge into the middle of things: "I want to tell you how deeply I regret my failure and the failure of my race and my class to support this nation during the time of its development these past fifteen years. We have stood aside, wrapped in our pride and resentment, refusing to offer the hand of experience that might have proved helpful."

There was silence and I thought to myself that I'd sounded like a minister in his pulpit.

"My father asked for your help," Jan said slowly. "We needed you Austrians. It was his dream that the races should live together. Father has always said that we must 'build a sort of Switzerland,' with its wealth of different cultures. But right now we don't look like a Switzerland in the making. These confounded Germans are making it damned difficult!"

We were talking in English and I realized with a twinge of amusement that to them I appeared more American than Austrian. Perhaps, too, my admitting my Austrian failings had given Jan the liberty to express his feelings.

"I know," I responded. "I've been reading your father's matchless aims and ambitions for our country. But he must know that these can never be fulfilled unless people like me and my kind accept responsibility for dealing with the corrosive emotions that divide Austrian from Czech and Czech from Slovak. I want you to know that my wife and I have dedicated our lives to the healing of these rifts."

Olga's face was alight with warmth and understanding; Alice leaned over and gently pressed Dorothy's hand and said, "You, my dear, are American and you are young. You must surely be confused by our medieval manners and customs."

My wife spoke out firmly. "Dr. Alice, yes, we are very brash and inclined to think we have all the answers. But many of us do care about other countries, as I now care about Czechoslovakia. But it's only recently that I began to see how shallow I've been in my thinking. I do hope that Gene and I, as an Austro-American couple, can be of some use."

Jan leapt to his feet. "I want to take Gene to meet Father!"

"No, Jan," said Alice anxiously, "he's too weak for any excitement. You understand, Mr. Teuber."

"He can be brief," said Jan firmly. "Father needs things to feed his spirit."

I suggested that we go upstairs and I would wait outside the room while Jan spoke to his father. It was agreed, and I found myself pacing up and down a corridor, my thoughts in turmoil. At last Jan came out, closed the door gently, shaking his head.

"Father was very touched. He had tears in his eyes. Your apology and your decision – they meant so very much to him. He asked me to thank you for coming and bringing him hope. Not many people do."

Jan said his father had sighed and added that he only wished more of the Austrians – and the Czechs – could feel as the Teubers did. That would give strength to the nation and to democracy.

Jan looked at me steadily: "Father said to me as I left, 'As things are, I fear for our future.' "

His words were only too prophetic, and more so than I could realize at the time — for our country and for his family and mine.

We returned to the terrace and sat talking about past and future. Jan was still under the spell of his father's forebodings and he launched into a recital of Tomáš Masaryk's dealings with us Austrians over the years.

It was old history to me, but new to Dorothy: At the beginning of the century, he said, his father, then a member of the Austrian Parliament, had often repeated a Czech historian's dictum that if Austria had not existed it would have had to be created in order to protect the various national groups in Central Europe from takeover by the Germans or the Russians. But by the beginning of World War I in 1914 Masaryk had become disenchanted with the Austrian ruling classes and started to work for dismemberment of the Austro-Hungarian Empire.

"That old Austrian Monarchy and nobility had a lot of charm," said Jan, "but, Gene, I remember Father saying that the only real concern of your princes, counts and barons in the Upper Houses of the Parliaments in Vienna, Bohemia and Moravia was to make sure that the sessions never fell during the hunting season and interfered with their all-important shoots!"

Jan added that he himself had acquired a firsthand knowledge of the Austrian nobility while serving among their ranks in the military and diplomatic corps. "I can tell you it was the ultimate disaster for them," he said with a laugh, "if there weren't enough stags, roebuck or chamois for every titled son to shoot at least one of those noble animals! I'm exaggerating, but that was a symptom of their failure to think beyond their own concerns to the welfare of the whole country. Let's face it, Gene, the time was ripe for a free and independent Czechoslovakia."

I laughed too, if a little wryly, and put up no defense.

But I wanted to leave the Masaryks with some hope for the future. I said, "Real democracy, whose origins I saw in America, the kind your father was determined to build, is possible, but only at the price of some basic changes in the way people live. But isn't it far more costly to live in a world without those essential personal changes?"

We talked for a little longer, but I found it discouraging that when the need for change was discussed, the family kept coming back to the menace of Hitler and his Germany. It seemed as if the Germans had now stepped into the shoes of the Austrians as the one people who needed to be different.

We said our cordial goodbyes and back at the Hotel Excelsior I found a message from Papa that he had sent his car and chauffeur to bring us home. When we had left that morning he had pointedly not offered a car and we had had to make our own way to Prague. On the drive back I was glad to have the opportunity to talk with our chauffeur Karmazín, whom I had known so well when we had played together as children. At first he barely replied to my questions, but when I told him about our visit with the Masaryks and their concern for the future of the country he loosened up.

"They should be concerned," he said. When I asked him why, he came back with: "A lot is wrong. Agrarian reform, for example, is all right as far as it's gone, but it hasn't gone nearly far enough. Many farmers don't have enough machines, nor enough cattle. Pardon my mentioning it, Honored Sir, but when the government took some of your lands, the bureaucrats began lining their own pockets and the people always come out on the short end."

As Karmazín spat out his feelings his foot pressed more heavily on the accelerator and we were soon whizzing down the highway. Some of the country's leaders might have started with good intentions, he said, but now the spouting democrats were lording it over the plain people. "If I may say so, Sir, they look down on us worse than your people do! And as for that Beneš – rumor has it that he's become a 'lordly gentleman' with an estate!''

We laughed. Then I told him a little more of our conversation with the Masaryks. He was plainly astonished. ''You, the son of a large estate owner, said that to a Czech president! Well, Sir, you were always more democratic than the rest, and then marrying an American lady.'' A long silence, then, ''But the others won't change.''

A melancholy mood descended on him and he remained silent for the rest of the drive.

Peace or War?

DOROTHY AND I returned to San Francisco and there our second son Anthony (Tony) was born. Then, after much deliberation we decided to take up our inheritance and settle with our two sons in Czechoslovakia. Our whole family moved to Křižanov in July, 1936. Our decision had been weighed carefully because the future of Europe was becoming increasingly clouded. In March, 1936, Hitler had reoccupied the Rhineland, violating the terms of the Versailles Treaty. The Western powers, Britain, France, Belgium and Italy, as well as the League of Nations, had denounced the action, but applied no sanctions. The government in Prague reacted by constructing a series of fortifications along its border with Germany.

It was now more than two years later, and once more Czechoslovakia was in the news. Hitler's troops had marched into Vienna in March, 1938, without resistance and he had annexed Austria. So our country was now surrounded on three sides by Germany. In April, Konrad Henlein, leader of the German-speaking people of the Sudetenland, the north-western territory of Czechoslovakia, demanded autonomy for that region. The Prague government rejected the demand and in May rushed troops to the German border.

Now, in the last days of August, Dorothy and I were paying a visit to Uncle Carl at his castle, only a few miles from the German border. Gathered there was a small but diverse group who reflected some of the conflicting interests in the confused international scene: our hosts, Uncle Carl and Aunt Biba, Austrian nobility, were staunch supporters of the German-speaking community; Aunt Biba's sister, Countess Irene Dubská, regarded herself as a realist, which meant in practice that she went along with the current mood of appeasement of Hitler; her son, Count Addi, was an outspoken champion of Henlein and Hitler. Also with us were Polish Ambassador Pavel, an articulate spokesman for democratic elements in Poland, and American Consul-General Bruins, with his transatlantic viewpoint.

We were crouched tensely around the radio in the library listening to the evening news. Three times daily households around the country could be found hanging on the news broadcasts. Tonight, August 27, we heard the measured cadences of Winston Churchill's prophetic words:

It is difficult for us . . . here, in the heart of peaceful law-abiding England to realize the ferocious passions which are rife in Europe. During these anxious months you have no doubt seen reports in the newspapers, one week good, another week bad; one week better, another week worse. But I must tell you that the whole state of Europe and of the world is moving steadily towards a climax which cannot be long delayed.

All of us in the room were all too aware of the imminent climax, a decision for war or peace, for dismemberment or a solution for our country.

Lord Runciman, Britain' unofficial mediator, was now the subject of the news, conferring between Henlein, the representative of the Sudeten German Party, and our President, Beneš. It seemed that their conflicting demands were irreconcilable. The broadcast over, our excited conversation was resumed.

"These newscasters are despicable," declared Uncle Carl, rising and standing before the fireplace, his favorite place for declaiming. "All this talk of the mobilizing of Czech forces – exaggerated! Hitler's ranting, Britain's indecisiveness – they are forever painting the situation as black as possible. They refuse to admit that we'll work out a solution."

Uncle considered himself a realist, but he was very selective in the facts he accepted. Now he turned to the Polish Ambassador. "Look, Pavel, in spite of that fellow Runciman's ignorance about our country I have a certain confidence in him; he's honest and he listens to our side. I was with him last week in Bohemia at Ulrich Kinský's place and we went over together to the Hohenlohes to meet with Henlein. It's the first time really that we German-speaking people are getting a fair hearing from those fuzzy idealists in the so-called democracies."

Without giving Pavel a chance to reply, Uncle Carl rambled on about Runciman; after all, he was *mein Herr*, just as Ulrich, Mappl, Pavel and himself – *mein Herr* signified more than a gentleman, it had a feudal tone to it; Ulrich was Prince Ulrich Kinský, Mappl was Prince Egon Hohenlohe, two of the largest landowners in Bohemia.

Pavel seized his chance to speak; "You know, Carl, one must make allowances for the English. The average gentleman in their conservative clubs actually believes it's possible to build a truly democratic society while still leaving him free to enjoy his 'natural privileges'. They are sincere hypocrites!"

We were startled by a smothered laugh from Dorothy. "What is it, darling?" I asked. The somber talk didn't seem to justify amusement. Dorothy said apologetically, "Hearing Prince Ulrich's name reminded me of that time we met him."

Everyone wanted to hear about it and Dot enlivened the serious atmosphere with her anecdote: When Gene's family and friends first heard of the engagement Papa had asked Prince Ulrich, who was making a trip around the world, to stop in San Francisco and find out what she was like. Ulrich had phoned Gene and invited him to dinner at the Palace Hotel. Gene had not only accepted, but in his carefree manner asked to include his fiancee at the meal. The Prince had wanted to know if Gene had his father's blessing on the engagement and Gene had blithely said yes.

"Gene explained to me Prince Ulrich's impressive social standing and I dressed discreetly for the occasion. There he was, awaiting us in the lobby, tall and dark, with those heavy brows and deep, penetrating eyes. I was astonished to see him wrapped in a long cloak lined in red and a stand-up collar. Beside him was his military aide, a Count, in gold braid and full military attire. They looked as though they'd stepped out of the pages of an historical novel."

My wife went on to describe how the Prince handed his cloak to the head waiter, who led them to a ringside table bedecked with red roses. At her place was a purple orchid which the waiter pinned on her shoulder. Ulrich and Gene were such good friends and the meal passed in delightful fashion, with Dorothy forgetting to remain on her best behavior.

Dorothy paused. "Yes, there was a sequel we heard about later. The Prince reported to Papa, who wanted to know all about his future daughter-in-law. It seems that Ulrich had said she was quite pretty and obviously well-bred and intelligent. Papa had beamed. But, Ulrich had added, "Of course, Eugene, she's American!"

Everyone laughed. "You haven't heard the best part," my wife added. "It was Papa himself who told me the story, and then roared with laughter and gave me a big hug!"

After this cheerful diversion our conversation returned to the international crisis. Pavel declared that informed sources had assured him that Lord Runciman had been launched by Chamberlain into what he called "that strange, far away Central European situation" as a mediator "in response to the request of the Czechoslovak government." But according to Pavel's sources, the government had never made such a request and Runciman's arrival was a total surprise.

Aunt Biba joined in. "I'm more than half English myself, but they still puzzle me at times. Runciman admitted to us at the Kinský's that when Chamberlain asked him to undertake the mission he'd remonstrated that he knew nothing about Czechoslovakia – 'You're setting me adrift in a small boat in mid-ocean!' he'd said. Chamberlain had just brushed this aside. So the poor man has been bouncing back and forth between Beneš and Henlein. It's my personal opinion that those English gentlemen assume they can't possibly go far wrong in dealing with such simple people as the Czechoslovaks!''

Ambassador Pavel spoke up: ''I think you have a point there, Countess. However, we Poles have much the same attitude towards the Czechs and to the Germans and Russians. In fact, to be honest, don't you and Carl feel the same way towards the Czechs?''

Uncle Carl stepped in crisply: ''Well, if we're going to be honest, let's face it. The Czechs came up from nothing. All they have is what we've made of them.''

That was too much for me. ''You say these lowly Czechs are what we, the great cultured Austrians, have made of them, which is not much, in your view. So what does that say about Austrian ability over the last three centuries?''

Uncle Carl chose to pass off my point with a laugh. ''You're nothing but a young American liberal.'' He was on his dignity now. He talked about his younger days as a civil servant in the office of the Governor of Bohemia. He'd had no trouble then dealing with the simple Czech people and always found them respectful. ''The only trouble I had was that they treated me with more respect as a Count than they did my boss.''

I was not to be put down. ''Uncle, you've just described the heart of the trouble. We landowners have never regarded the Czechs as equals; it's always been a master-servant relationship. We were in the castle and they were in the village. We've had the superior political and economic power and we've held on to it.''

''And we have a superior culture and in fact are a superior race,'' said Uncle impatiently. ''And that is why the present situation is so intolerable. All of us Austrians and Germans in this country, who share the same culture, deserve a better place in the sun. And we're going to get it!''

No one spoke and in the silence I could clearly hear the rumble of trucks and the steady tramp of heavy boots on the road bordering the estate. The Czech Army was again reinforcing the border.

After a minute, John Bruins, the American Consul General in Prague, who'd had little to say, commented, ''Looking at the European scene as an outsider, it seems to me that the Czechs have a long memory. They have not forgotten that in these Bohemian lands three centuries ago, until the Battle on the White Mountain, they were the masters. And now, because they feel themselves to be a part of the great western democratic tradition, they consider themselves called on to lead the Republic into a better future.''

He added that as an American he understood that sense of mission which, in fact, they had drawn in large measure from the United States. He drew a swift rejoinder from Uncle Carl, who said that if the Czechs regarded the way they'd been treating the Germans and Austrians, not to mention the Hungarians, Poles and even the Slovaks within their borders, as democracy and equality, then they were just a bunch of hypocrites. He added with some heat, ''And you Americans, Mr. Bruins, should hang your heads in shame that your pupils have made such a farce of your teachings.''

The Ambassador stepped in to ease the tension, ''I'm so glad, Carl, that you as a representative of the Gothic Holy Roman Empire deign to include us Poles among the superior peoples, though I doubt if Herr Hitler would agree with you.'' He added with a smile that while his patriotic and aristocratic soul longed to agree with Carl, his college days in Oxford and his diplomatic service in the Orient had taught him differently. ''There is no such thing as a pure race. We are all mongrels. Families like ours that pride ourselves on our long histories brought our mothers, wives and mistresses from every nation under the sun.''

That brought Countess Irene into the ring. ''All that may be true,'' she said, ''but realistically we have to recognize and deal with the quirks and evils in some peoples." For example, she said, the Germans had been forced to do something about the exploiting ways of the Jews. Those who were more intellectually and morally fit than others just had to assert their leadership. Why, even Plato and Aristotle didn't see equal rights for all citizens in a democracy.

Her son had been waiting his turn and he jumped in. "We young men who have inherited name and privilege have to play our part in creating a new order. One race or group within a nation must of necessity be dominant, otherwise you have chaos such as in Italy before Fascism or in Germany before National Socialism."

This was too much for Bruins, who asserted firmly that he saw no chaos in his own country's democracy. One simply had to learn how to make democracy operative, and that required a love of freedom without extreme individualism. The trouble in Italy and Germany was that no one felt responsible for the whole body politic, so when the political parties splintered it was only too easy for the dictators to step in and rule by force.

The arguments went back and forth, with Uncle Carl heading the authoritarian cause, citing everyone from Saint Francis of Assisi to Mussolini to provide support, while I fought him back in the cause of democracy with Saint Joan of Arc!

Returning to more recent times, Bruins affirmed that Tomáš Masaryk had stood in his day for moral authority. Pavel agreed with him, pointing out that at his death there was widespread grief all over Europe in tribute to his integrity.

Finally, our conversation was interrupted by the blare of a brass band and the lusty singing of male voices. A delegation from one of the nearby villages was serenading the household on the front porch. When we went out to meet them they presented Uncle Carl and Aunt Biba with cakes and wine and invited them to a forthcoming "Kirchentag," a church day assembly.

As all of us, together with the servants, stepped out on to the sandy square in front of the entrance the band struck up a waltz. Responding to the occasion Uncle slipped an arm around the only girl in the band and whirled her into a dance. Immediately the husky young peasants in their local costumes, green jackets, alpine leather pants, feathered hats – and white stockings (sign of their membership in Henlein's Sudeten German Party), bowed low to the ladies of the house and the servant girls. In no time a ball was in progress at three o'clock in the afternoon.

The care-free scene seemed all the stranger to my eyes as I watched these country boys dancing the waltz and polka. I was very well aware that many of them would be drafted any day and would have to exchange their colorful costumes for the hated grey Czech army uniforms. This very night the chauffeur and one of the grooms would be leaving this house to join their military units because of the partial mobilization. An ugly mood had descended on this part of the country as divided loyalties were becoming more evident. A few days earlier a strict order from Henlein to all the Sudeten German organizations not to provoke incidents with Czechs had been cancelled.

Now these white-stockinged youths had begun hurling insults at passing troops. The soldiers, who had been ordered not to retaliate, could only glare back. It was a serious question how long order could be maintained, and I, for one, suspected that Henlein, and Hitler behind him, would be happy to see the outbreak of 'border incidents.'

I was concerned that Uncle Carl and Aunt Biba were deeply involved in this confrontation. They had been in close touch with Henlein and the Sudeten German Party for the past three years. They had even taken him to London in 1935 and again this May to meet, through Aunt's relatives, with men in the government close to the British Prime Minister. Uncle Carl had explained to me that their hope was that they might give direction to the movement. When I expressed my belief that Henlein was following Hitler's game plan, Uncle maintained that Henlein was being forced into alliance with the Fuhrer by the lack of leadership and hesitant tactics of Beneš. Whatever the rights and wrongs of the situation, it was only too apparent that most of our country was in the grip of a resigned apathy, with disaster ahead.

The following Sunday Uncle Carl invited me to go with him to the "Kirchentag" fiesta in a village ten miles away. We drove over dirt roads in his flashy white Alfa Romeo at such a pace that everyone made way for us. Uncle was the featured speaker and would lead the parade. At the edge of the village we mounted two thoroughbred jumpers that had been sent ahead from his stables. Following us in the parade came the scions of the large farmers of the area astride plough horses, curried and spruced up for the occasion. We dismounted in front of the church and after Holy Mass marched to the platform set up in the center of the village where some four thousand people were assembled to listen to the speeches.

Several bland exhortations were given by clergy – all had been admonished by the Bishop not to touch on anything political; then came equally unctuous words from the mayor and several Sudeten politicians. Then "Our Sir Count" mounted the rostrum and was greeted with cheers. He started with "My very honored lady comrades and dear comrades, we are all angry with the Czechs, aren't we?" Great applause. "And we all are convinced that they have treated us badly, although we are superior to them in culture, tradition and manhood." The crowd yelled bravos.

"I am not going to talk about the Czechs or the injustices we have suffered, but I shall tell you just what our manhood should be and how our culture and tradition bid us live."

He went on to quote Goethe's dictum that those periods of history in which faith dominates are the ones that are brilliant and uplifting to the heart, and he told them simply how their faith must carry them through to victory. He warned them that their fate depended on their own faith and not on how others treated them. "It is our homes that must create the manhood and the culture that our country needs. Then you will create your own future and the Czechs will be grateful to you."

Some of the speech was no doubt over the heads of his listeners, but his challenge to them to live up to their best principles with integrity was not lost on them and they gave him a rousing ovation. Sadly the times were already too stressful; this village and many others around it were on the brink of a flood that was to carry all before it.

Awaiting me at Uncle's house was a telegram urgently requesting my presence in Geneva. Ever since my return to Czechoslovakia in 1933 I'd been involved with the growing number of men and women associated with the Oxford Group, the movement that had made such an impact on my wife and me in San Francisco. Among the countries to which they had brought a new spirit of honesty and reconciliation was Norway. So many people there had paid their taxes in full that the government had to readjust its budget to make use of the excess revenue.

Now, it seemed, the President of the Norwegian Parliament, Carl Hambro, had invited representatives from several countries to speak at a luncheon in Geneva, where he was a prominent figure in the League of Nations. Leaders of the League and members of the diplomatic corps were expected at the occasion, and here was a request for me to join the panel of speakers.

In his invitation to his fellow diplomats Hambro stressed that his reason for bringing them together was that "we have felt that in this hour of grave apprehension and fear it is of vital importance to meet hope and faith and strength. We have the impression that these people have succeeded in fundamental things where we have failed."

He could not have chosen a more dramatic moment for the event. It was scheduled for a few days ahead, September 15, 1938. On that day British Prime Minister Chamberlain was to meet with Hitler at Berchtesgaden to discuss the Czech crisis. His plan was to cede to Germany areas where more than half the population was in favor of that *Anschluss*. Included in that territory was the place I was now visiting.

When I showed the telegram to Uncle Carl he was for once deadly serious. "Genus, of course you must go. Your friends need you. But please understand that Biba and I can't be responsible for your wife and children for long. Chamberlain is on his way to Hitler and Henlein is already there. Biba and I would be the first to be taken away if anything goes wrong – pray God it won't."

Next morning I left for Switzerland and two days later Dorothy and the boys followed.

9

Family Break

IN THE COURSE OF the month after Dorothy and I left for Geneva, the fateful meeting took place in Munich between Chamberlain, Mussolini, Daladier of France and Hitler and the Nazis acquired ten thousand square miles of Czechoslovakian territory, with its nearly three million German-speaking inhabitants as well as 700,000 Czechs. In addition to that loss, my country was further carved up by the Poles occupying the Teschen area and by Slovakia and Ruthenia each being granted full autonomy.

In the autumn of 1938 Dorothy and I returned to a dispirited land. It seemed to me that Hitler, far from being satisfied with his gains, was making his plans for further eastward expansion, but Papa, although clearly concerned about what was happening, maintained an optimistic calm. He even expressed a belief that the Austrian Czechs, with their influence in the Sudeten Party, could steer events in a positive direction.

The only positive development that I could see in Europe was that at long last Britain and France had been shaken out of their mood of appeasement and were seriously stepping up their military rearmament. At this time my colleagues in the Oxford Group were campaigning for a moral and spiritual rearmament to undergird the strength of the democracies. They argued that physical rearmament alone was no match for the challenge of the totalitarian states, which reinforced their arms with the ideological commitment of their peoples. The press reported this theme so widely that the Oxford Group came to be known as Moral Re-Armament.

A campaign of letters written by respected British leaders in several walks of life advocating Moral Re-Armament was published in *The Times* of London and commanded wide attention. Its theme was that "the strength of a nation consists in the vitality of her principles. Policy is for every nation ultimately determined by the character of her people and by the acceptance in their lives of honesty, faith and love as the foundations on which a new world may be built. Without these qualities, the strongest armaments, the most elaborate pacts, only postpone the hour of reckoning." These letters were followed by a number of radio broadcasts culminating in a series of talks over Europe's powerful Radio Luxembourg.

On a cold February evening in 1939 Dorothy and I were playing a game of bridge with Mama and Papa at Křižanov. Outside, snow lay thick on the ground, but here in the library a roaring fire kept the room cosy. The mounted roebuck heads on the walls looked down with much the same serious expression as the four of us scanning our cards around the table. Papa and Dorothy had just made a little slam. The door opened and Maroush, the footman entered, bearing a silver tray. Papa looked up, frowning at this unexpected interruption, but it was to me that Maroush proffered the tray. On it was a telegram that was to change the course of my life.

I opened it and read its contents aloud. It was an urgently worded request for Dorothy and me to come to Paris this coming week to take part in those radio broadcasts arranged by Radio Luxembourg. My words were greeted by an icy silence. I was not altogether surprised, since Papa and I had talked several times about my future. I had come from America with the conviction that I should prepare myself for the responsibilities of running the estates when Papa turned over my inheritance to me. He had questioned my frequent participation in the programs of Moral Re-Armament on the grounds that they interfered with my duties at Křižanov. Evidently this one was one too many.

"The time has come for you to choose!" Papa spoke up sternly, fixing my eye across the card table.

"Genus, this castle has stood here for close to a thousand years and I expect it to stand for a few centuries longer. These lands have been in your family for several generations. It has taken me almost fifty years to build them into the model estates they have become."

He leaned towards me. "If you insist on going to Paris to try to save the world with these new ideas of yours and neglect the management of these lands – this sacred property which I have expected to entrust to you as my eldest son – then I am telling you here and now that I will have to disinherit you. You will be out and your brother will take over."

I was stunned and sat trying to put my thoughts in order. There had been hints of Papa's impatience at my absences and my failure to devote my entire attention to the estates. Unconsciously my mind must have weighed the competing demands of a continent and nation in turmoil and of the care and development of the properties; but until now I had not been brought up against a fundamental choice.

"Well?" Papa's terse question shattered the silence.

"I must think, Papa. May I give you my answer in the morning?"

He rose and with his customary affection and courtesy kissed Dorothy's hand and I kissed Mama's and Papa's hands and cheeks. Mani, who had been a spectator of all this, looked at me with troubled compassion as we bade each other goodnight.

Dorothy and I slept little that night as we struggled for wisdom to make the right decision. Papa's sudden ultimatum brought a pang to my heart as I faced the prospect of relinquishing Křižanov; a stream of memories flashed through my mind – a deer with her two fawns sipping water from a pond in the pale light of evening; the golden buds of wheat bursting through their green sheaths; the mysterious tunnels stretching beneath the castle, waiting to be explored; the irresistible aroma of hot baked bread wafting from the kitchen; the row of smiling faces of the staff lined up to greet me on my return home.

Křižanov was a large part of me. Never had I been so aware of my dreams that out of the mingling of feudal tradition and modern technology I would somehow build a pattern of justice, peace and plenty for all who lived in that beautiful place. Was I crazy to throw it all away? Was I truly deserting my basic responsibilities, as Papa believed? Was I denying my sons their birthright?

But outside our gates stood a world in disarray. Other estates like ours had already been taken over by ambitious men and greedy governments. And not just feudal land, but industries, cities and nations. My country was being inexorably squeezed by tyrants to the east and west. In the midst of the madness in the world Dorothy and I had encountered men and women whose thinking and living were in contrast to the control of the dictatorships and the apathy of the democracies; we had seen the electric response to a message of wholehearted commitment to a firm faith in God's direction in the affairs of men.

The issue before us was whether we were prepared to join our voices and our allegiance to the battle to save what we held dear in the world. The choice lay beyond our reasoning, and as we sat watching the first light of dawn filter through the drapes and heard the peal of bells for early vespers my wife and I came to a decision. Heavy-hearted but sure, we joined the family for breakfast.

"Please understand, Papa," I pleaded. "We are in a world emergency and we must play our part. I feel that high as the cost may seem, should we not respond, the cost may be far higher. And, Papa, should we not succeed, you too may lose all you hold dear."

"Nonsense!" retorted Papa. "You exaggerate the dangers." He went on to argue that the worst crisis had passed and all the Führer wanted was to build peace. He wished he could convince me that I should stay right here and make the most of the opportunities we Austrians had in the Sudeten Party. "Your duty is at Křižanov, not off fighting for a dream. If you go now, this must be a parting of the ways."

Papa's face was ravaged and I knew his words were torn from deep in his heart. He added more quietly, "In any case, I trust you are leaving Jerry and Tony here for the time being?"

We nodded. Dorothy was expecting the birth of our third son before long and we had made plans for the birth in Brno.

The decision to leave for Paris had been made, but now came the practical question of how to make the journey. In March, 1939, leaving or entering a country was no simple matter; exit permits and visas were strictly controlled here in Europe. Even more of a problem for us at this moment was the question of money. I had left my work in America and was receiving no income; our modest savings were gone; Papa's small stipend was at an end, and I could not now ask for his help.

I made travel arrangements, ordering train tickets from Prague to Paris for the tenth of March, still not knowing where the money to pay for them would come from. We planned to stop off in Prague to visit Foreign Minister Chvalkovský for last minute news and advice, especially reassurance that it was safe to leave the children behind. I had become acquainted with him through his Belgian-French-Swiss wife.

On the morning before we were due to leave, Miruš was at work packing my clothes; down the hall in the nursery Jerry and Tony were racing their trains up and down the carpet while their excellent governess knitted a Tyrolean sweater for one of them. We knew they would be happy with the household in our absence. Jerry was already bilingual in German and English; Tony mostly chattered away in German.

Franz came into the room with the mail. I opened an envelope bearing English stamps, addressed in a hand I did not recognize. The letter read:

Dear Mr. Teuber: At the luncheon given by President Carl Hambro in Geneva last September I heard you speak. Your words stressing the answer to hate as the solution to the Sudeten crisis as well as your conception of the role minorities might play in the development of a nation impressed me very much.

I am enclosing a check for £200 for you to use in the work you are doing. I obtained your name from friends in London.

With every good wish for the success of your efforts.

Dorothy and I were stunned. £200 was the exact amount we needed for the tickets.

We were invited to lunch by Minister and Mrs. Chvalkovský in the sumptuous baroque Czernin Palace, the Ministry of Foreign Affairs, where they had their living quarters. The palace had a tragic history from the beginning; it had been built some two centuries earlier by a count for his adored wife, but she had died just before it was completed and he had refused to live there. Here, too, tragedy would soon overtake our host, and later still, the body of our friend Jan Masaryk would fall through the very window where the Minister was now standing, pointing out to us the beauties of the view.

Luncheon today, however, was impeccably served, and our hosts were relaxed and cheerful. Over coffee the Minister mused about his experiences in Rome, where he had served as ambassador, and in Berlin. In Italy he had seen the early years of Fascism and in Germany the birth of Nazism, and had come away still believing that they signalled a rebirth for their nations.

Today Chvalkovský was no longer as convinced that Mussolini and Hitler were simply the champions of order amidst decadent and confused democratic politicians. But when I asked him bluntly about rumors that Hitler would seize the fateful "Ides of March" to move into Czechoslovakia, he assured us, "No, certainly not. Hitler is in exactly the position we want him. He wants to woo and win our country. He will not move. You can travel in peace of mind.''

Madame Chvalkovská added ''My husband understands Herr Hitler. I think your children are safe in your beautiful place.'' Dorothy and I felt she was not quite as confident as her husband.

''Why, I speak to him or his Minister here in Prague every day,'' our host added. ''My understanding of him enables me to handle him. Don't worry.''

Certainly life seemed to be going on as normal in Prague as we drove to the station and boarded our train for Paris. Dorothy peered out of the window at the spires of Hradshin castle and the winding streets of the old city as I settled in to work on my forthcoming radio talk. Before our train steamed into Paris next day events were unfolding that would drastically change the history of my country.

Today was March 10, 1939. Unbeknownst to us, the Prague Government was in the act of deposing Slovak Premier Tiso on the charge of working for the autonomy of Slovakia. Next day Hitler promised Tiso his support, and on March 14 summoned President Emil Hácha, a kindly but frail old man, together with our friend František Chvalkovský to Berlin. Next day Hitler demanded that they sign a pledge placing the Czech people ''trustingly in the hands of the Führer.''

The two men protested that they had no authority to do such a thing, but the following day the Czech Parliament, feeling unable to withstand the pressure, agreed. On the fifteenth Hitler proclaimed Bohemia-Moravia under his protection. Next day he arrived in Prague and the following day was in Brno. German military poured across the country. Neither France nor England had raised a murmur in our defense.

In Paris we looked at the huge headlines announcing Hitler's appearance in Prague and telling of the military occupation of our Moravia. We tried in vain to communicate with Křižanov; telephone, radio and rail communication with Czechoslovakia was cut. The French people with whom we talked were angry, frightened and bewildered.

We went at once to the office of U.S. Ambassador William Bullitt, who was a close friend of Dorothy's family, and found him pacing up and down, bitterly enraged at what he termed Hitler's perfidy. He had received no advance intelligence reports of the imminence of the take-over. We explained to the Ambassador our predicament and our deep concern for our two sons. We speculated on whether the Czech countryside would accept the inevitable, or whether perhaps Czechs in the villages might even use this opportunity to turn against their German and Austrian land-owners. We asked the Ambassador how we could find out what was happening.

Bullitt clenched and unclenched his fists in impotent rage. "I wish to God I could help you, but I have no means of communication. The situation frankly is in the hands of a madman."

Dorothy and I were shaken. Our immediate concern was for the children and how to get them out of the country. My wish was to go back, leaving Dorothy in Paris, since she was pregnant, but I was Czech and I travelled on a Czech passport. Every Czech was now being urgently ordered to return to the country and I knew very well that I would not be allowed out again. There was the further problem that since my parents were active in the Sudeten German Party there was every likelihood that they were automatically incorporated into the Nazi Party, and there was no telling what my status would be.

Dorothy, on the other hand, was an American citizen and had her American passport and would be able to leave Czechoslovakia with the children. I was most reluctant for her to go, but she was so obsessed with the boys' predicament that she seemed to have no fear of making the journey.

Then we had to confront the problem that there was no means of travel. For three weeks, still without news from the family, we went every day to the travel agency. Sorry, there were no trains crossing the border, and in any case Madame had no military permit to enter the Moravian Protectorate.

Dorothy was determined to obtain such a permit and paid a call on the German consulate. There she was received with courtesy and produced her passport. The official studied it and asked the nationality of her husband. When she admitted that I held a Czech passport he announced that I would be granted the honor of German citizenry and she would not then need a military permit. All that was necessary was for her to provide him with my address, and of course I should return to my homeland immediately. Hurriedly Dorothy thanked him and propelled her six-month pregnant frame out of the consulate. Forget the permit!

Then came news from Křižanov. Papa cabled, "Boys well. All well. Hope you return soon."

One morning we both had a clear sense that this day Dorothy would leave for Prague and I helped her pack her bag. When we entered the travel agency the man behind the counter greeted us as usual with "No further news as yet," and repeated his customary litany about no trains, travel was not recommended, the agency could take no responsibility.

Dorothy spoke up quietly, "Sir, if you had two young children at this moment under Nazi occupation what would you do? I must have your help."

The man looked at her silently and at length said, "Madame, I fear for you, and it is not our policy, since it may not help you, but I will issue the ticket to Prague and you must take your chances on how far it will get you."

We said farewells to our friends and headed for the train station. When I helped her aboard the sleeper car for Eger, the German-Czech border town, we found Dorothy was the only passenger. Dealing firmly with the fear in both our hearts, we embraced and parted.

10

Perilous Journey
Dorothy's Account

FOR AS LONG AS I COULD I fastened my eyes on Gene's sturdy figure until the train slid into the murky tunnel at the end of the platform. He seemed the last remaining security in a crumbling world. Then, as the baby moved jerkily within me I settled my bulk into a seat in the empty compartment.

"Votre passeport, Madame." A friendly conductor appeared at my side. "I'll keep it for you along with your currency for declaration at the border. It's safer with me," he added ominously. I did as he said, wondering what he would say when he found I had no military permit. But somewhere deep within me I felt a confidence that everything would work out.

I fell asleep. Much later I was awakened by a brusque voice in German announcing we had reached the border. I looked out to see we were already at Eger, the German-Czech frontier. Standing on the platform were three men wearing heavy blue capes with brass buttons and shining steel helmets. I realized that they were studying my green American passport. One of them came up the steps and entered the compartment.

"You have no military permit," he said abruptly. "This border is under military control. You must leave the train immediately."

"This train continues to Prague?" I asked. Wonder of wonders! I had been told it went no further than Eger.

He said with a note of pride, "The Führer has brought order, and today we are permitting trains to cross. Now, Madame, this way, please."

"No," I said firmly, "I must go on to Prague."

He hesitated. "Madame is American. You have perhaps properties in Prague?"

"No," I said reluctantly. "But I have children outside Prague."

He left me and I watched in suspense as he talked with his colleagues. He returned to say, "Madame, you must leave the train. We have checked the regulations and 'children' are not included in the category of 'valuables'." He reached for my arm to assist me.

"No!" I said, settling more firmly into my corner. He looked at me uncertainly and then joined his fellow police. Once again they huddled over my passport. Then an inspiration hit me. I rose and stood against the window, where my bulk was clearly outlined. Swathed in my cape and coat, triplets seemed imminent. I saw the policemen stare at me and glance at the bleak, snow-covered scene emerging in the twilight. I fancied I could hear the debate in their heads – which would their Führer require – undeviating obedience to regulations or avoidance of an international incident provoked by an intransigent lady?

One of them came aboard and said gruffly, "You may proceed, Madam," thrust my passport and a pass at me, turned and left.

My heart sang. Suddenly I felt very hungry, but alas there was no diner on the train. Never mind – what amazing fortune – this was the first train permitted to cross the border! Three hours later we steamed into Prague. Gene had telegraphed ahead for reservations for me at the Hotel Alcron, where we always stayed. I began to feel more secure.

The conductor appeared and handed down my luggage. I thanked him and asked for my currency back. He counted out in marks about one third of the sum I had turned over to him. I asked for the remainder, mindful that when I left Czechoslovakia I would be permitted to take out no more than I had brought in. Vehemently, the conductor asserted that this was all I had given him. As he stared glassily ahead I hailed a porter, who picked up my luggage. As I followed him, I was surrounded by a crowd of people beseeching me in English, French and German to exchange their Czech kronen for pounds, francs or marks. Pathetic Jewish faces engulfed me. They were imploring me to save their lives. Alas, I had barely enough money for my needs. As the throng pressed in on me I became afraid for my baby.

The strong arm of a taxi driver grasped me firmly and hoisted me into his cab. As we swung up in front of the Alcron I was startled to see police with steel helmets standing on either side of the entrance. A familiar clerk at the desk glanced at me with a harried look as he talked with a high-ranking officer. Finally I had his attention.

"Frau Baronin," he welcomed me. "Indeed I received the Baron's telegram, but alas there is not one room available. This is the headquarters hotel for the German Military Command."

I looked around the lobby. There were soldiers everywhere. "All right," I said, accepting the inevitable. "But what I'm most anxious for is news of my children. Would you be kind enough to phone Schloss Křižanov, so that I can talk to them?"

I sat in the lobby, prepared for a long wait. Telephones in Křižanov were like those I recalled from my earliest youth – you cranked a wall phone and eventually a voice answered as from a far distance. Sometimes you reached your party and sometimes they could hear you. I ordered a sandwich and a milk from a busy waiter. After an hour I approached the busy clerk. "No response yet?"

"Gnädige Frau," he stammered, "Oh, Gnädige Frau, I have had a reply, but I couldn't bear to tell you."

My heart stopped and my knees began to shake. "Yes?"

"Your castle is evacuated and your children are gone."

I stumbled back to my seat and stared dazedly at the tufted red cushions. Whatever should I do? A clear, quiet voice sounded in my heart. "Don't worry. It's not true." The thought seemed illogical, but a calm settled on my turbulent spirits. I looked at my watch — ten o'clock. I asked the clerk to phone the American Embassy. Sorry, he said, your Embassy has been vacated.

I asked him to call a cab and he found me a driver who spoke German and instructed him to tour the hotels. We went rattling over the wet cobblestones from one hotel to another — all full of German officers. At last we came to one with a room, but the driver was adamant — no place for a lady.

Near exhaustion, I began to cry quietly. Suddenly a clear thought came to me. "Drive to the American Embassy," I said. Gene and I had paid a short visit to Ambassador Wilbur Carr and his wife on our way to Paris. I directed the cabbie to the Carr residence.

I could see a gleam of light inside the house and rang the bell hesitantly. The door opened and I saw Mrs. Carr. "You are here!" I cried.

Astonished at this apparition on her doorstep, she said, "Yes, but only just! Come in! We meant to leave this afternoon, but my husband was detained at the last moment. How did you know?"

She welcomed me in and I poured out my story to her and her husband. After a while the Ambassador got up and quietly left the room. Mrs. Carr insisted that I spend the night with them. The servants had gone to bed, but she found a box of blankets and we unpacked them and made my bed. To this day the smell of mothballs in wool brings me a wave of comfort and security.

The Ambassador returned. "Come and sit down," he said, "I have news for you. I still have some pull in this sick country. I was able to reach Schloss Křižanov; your family is there and the children are safe!"

"Then why . . ." I stammered.

"The Germans are an efficient lot. They've taken over your castle for their headquarters in the area because of the air strip nearby. The local telephone exchange has been told to answer all calls to Schloss Křižanov the way you were told. The Germans have their own military lines." Then he said with a grin, "I've asked that your car be here for you at ten tomorrow morning. Hope that's all right."

I could have hugged him. Later, as I stretched out in bed waiting for sleep, a procession of figures and faces paraded before me – the stern steel-helmeted police, the piteous expressions and grasping hands of the Jews at the station, my two-faced conductor – and I was overwhelmed by God's goodness to me.

Punctually at ten o'clock our family chauffeur Karmazín drove up in Papa's immaculate car and as I sank back into its cushioned seat I peppered him with questions. First the family news. Karmazín assured me that Papa and Mama and the children were well. Then he stopped, and as we drove through the outskirts of Prague I became fearful. What was he holding back?

"Gnädige Frau, you are American. You love your country, and we love ours. We have lost it. The Westerners who helped us found our democracy have deserted us. They have let a beast into our midst. They smiled and shook our hands and welcomed us to their conference tables and their trade agreements; now they have closed their eyes to our plight. We are like a helpless child, left wounded in a ditch while the bastard German soldiers march in to pick it up."

I was stunned by the molten bitterness pouring out of him. Karmazín, with his round, pink-cheeked, smooth face, always so friendly and courteous! Was this how all Czechoslovakia felt about the take-over? Slowly he started to tell me what had been happening. He had been asked to drive Papa and Mama, along with Jerry, to Brno to watch the arrival of German troops. The troops, it turned out, were Austrian soldiers, sent to march into town at 6 a.m. "to preserve peace and put down any disturbances that might endanger their brothers of the Sudeten-German minority."

Jerry had asked Karmazín to lift him up so he could see the troops. He had hoisted the grandson of his master on to his shoulders to watch the parade. I could imagine the violent feelings that had coursed through the obedient servant. I ached for him and wished my poor German could have conveyed to him all I felt.

There was a faint sneer in Karmazín's voice as he went on to tell how the commanding officer of nearly one hundred soldiers had presented himself to Papa at Křižanov. "The Herr Baron is still the head of his house," said Karmazín, "but the Commandant explained 'respectfully' that during this peaceful occupation he himself would be in charge!" The commandant had gone on to "request" that the troops be billeted in the offices and quarters around the courtyard and that the fifteen officers – all Austrians – be included at the family's meal table.

I didn't have the heart to ask Karmazín for more and we drove in silence through the brooding forest land until we reached the lakes and woods of Křižanov. I felt I was coming home as I glimpsed the castle's cream-colored facade with the red turrets at each corner – Gene called them architecturally poor, but I loved them. Two men servants threw open the gates and I caught my breath as I saw the courtyard ringed with soldiers lounging against the walls or leaning on their guns. Then my eye was held by two chubby little figures in their *Lederhosen*, goose-stepping in unison with a file of grey-clad helmeted troops. My blond, curly-headed babies, applauded by laughing soldiers!

The boys piled into my arms. The men all came to attention and gave me a disciplined "Heil Hitler!" I raised my hand in a vague gesture and bundled the children up the stairs to our family quarters. There I was besieged by questions – where is Daddy? Why did I come back without him? Why was Křižanov so full of soldiers? Why did they say "Heil Hitler" instead of "Gruss Gott"? As the maid unpacked and the governess left, the boys quieted.

"Mother," asked Jerry solemnly, "are these good soldiers?"

I quibbled. "Well, I don't know." I realized these were

the first soldiers the children had ever seen.

"I wasn't sure they were *very* good," Jerry went on thoughtfully, "because they came when Grosspapa and Grossmama didn't invite them. And you weren't here either, Mama. So I translated 'Onward Christian Soldiers' into German and sang it to the Kapitan."

I imagined with delight the expression on the face of the Kapitan as he was confronted by a six-year-old shouldering his responsibility.

Mani and Alice came in and gave me a joyful welcome, but then I was initiated into the artificial atmosphere in which they were living. Mani went over and picked pillows off the bed and placed one over the phone in my room and the other over the phone in the salon. Then, pointing up at the crystal chandelier, he draw me to a corner and said softly, "Dorothy, be careful of every word you say here. This place is full of informers, please believe me. I'm not being over fearful. I'm going to help you in every way I can to get out. But please realize that Papa and Mama will be your greatest blocks. They believe what they want to. They swallow all of Hitler's promises.

"The Germans have promised to restore all of our property confiscated by the Government." Mani smiled grimly, knowing his father's weakness.

So I was somewhat prepared for all the questions fired at me by my parents-in-law after their affectionate greetings. Why hadn't Gene come? Why must I go just as peace was descending on the country? What did people abroad think? What did I think?

In the salon before dinner Papa proudly displayed his American daughter-in-law to six young Austrian officers, who politely bent over my hand. The Kapitan was absent that evening. Then came more questions, sincerely asked, but hard to answer: We understand that Frau Baronin has just come from Paris. Could you explain why the French – and the British – are so critical of the Führer? Don't they see the peace he is building? Don't they realize that without him we would soon be at war?

At dinner I sat next to a very young, blond lieutenant from a small village in the Austrian Tyrol. With all the fervor of his youth he tried to make me understand Hitler's virtues – so like a father, such a teacher of gentlemanly behavior as well as soldiering. He himself, for example, came from a very simple background, but here he was, at ease sitting at an elegant table such as this.

After dinner came the real nightmare, when over our coffee Papa turned on the radio. What a blast of fury came forth, directed at that "red-haired little b . . . . . who sits on top of the hill." Eduard Beneš was the target of the vitriol. Beneš had succeeded to the presidency, but had resigned after the Munich debacle. The raucous voice continued its harangue about the peace-loving Germans and the rapacious Czechs, then switched to the saintly role of Hitler. I watched with sadness the dedicated looks of the officers, but with greater concern the expressions of satisfaction on the faces of Papa and Mama.

Day by day I watched the cumbersome German propaganda ground out to an unprotected nation and wondered how effective it was. Deserted by the West, betrayed by friends, divided by racial and cultural differences, the Czechs, I suspected, might fall prey to lies in the absence of truth in the news media. For three long weeks I endured this stifling atmosphere, only enlivened by the companionship of the boys. I had been in touch with my friend John Bruins, American Consul-General in Prague, about possible plans for leaving the country, but he had cautioned me to wait.

At night I often lay awake, hearing below my window the crunch of gravel under the feet of soldiers on their beat. I pictured their helmets and bayonetted guns. Down the long red-carpeted corridor was the nursery where the two boys were peacefully asleep. My thoughts so often turned to my husband and I rejoiced in the certainty and inner clarity he had brought into my life. One night I vividly relived our first encounter.

I had been looking out from the bedroom window of my home in Berkeley as my future brother-in-law, Edgar Gallwey, came walking up the garden path with a stranger. I was amused by the contrast between the two young men; Ed was New England to the core, tall, dark, steady and quiet. The stranger was shorter, blond, lithe and lean, with aquiline features, and he was talking eagerly, emphasizing his words with gestures of both hands. This must be the Austrian friend whom Ed had said he would bring to meet us.

As my sister Irene and I walked down the stairs I wondered if this Austrian would kiss my hand, and was a little disappointed when he didn't. Ed and Irene drifted off and Gene seated himself casually next to me on the couch. I liked the way he seemed to say whatever came into his mind – none of the calculated small talk I was used to. He had started right in telling me that Ed was angry with him, but he didn't look in the least sorry about it. It seemed that the world hero, Charles Lindbergh, fresh from his Atlantic flight, had come to stay with Gene's host in Burlingame and had offered to take Gene up in his plane for a few minutes. Ed was just jealous!

Then, with what I came to recognize as a typically swift change of mood, he went on, "I have so much to learn from your country. That Lindbergh, he says so little, but he is like an eager young eagle, determined to go higher and further than any of his kind. That is the spirit of America!" Then he had leaned towards me and asked if I believed in progress and started talking earnestly about Schopenhauer and Hegel. I was reading Michael Arlen and Walt Whitman at the time and felt totally out of my depth.

The next weeks had been easy and joyful. He started me reading with him the works of some of my country's great thinkers – Gene, who was deeply versed in European history, shamed me with his zest for American thought and literature. He was especially fascinated by Woodrow Wilson. "We Europeans often resent his idealism," said Gene, "but history may prove his 'unrealistic idealism' to be the means of rebirth for our old nations.''

The truly glowing days were those we spent in Carmel, that wonder spot of the Californian coast. My parents had invited him to join us there. We scrambled around the craggy paths of Point Lobos, through its wind-sculptured cypresses and above rocks and pools at the ocean's edge, where seals and otters played in the deep blue waters. Sitting in a crevice sheltered from the wind, we gazed at the scene, then turned to one another. That moment marked the birth of our understanding that Providence had made us for each other.

We had wandered back, a little sheepish, to confront my parents. I had told them I wasn't in love with Gene. Gene had left home with a stipend from Papa and his ringing instructions, ''You may do anything you wish, my son, except marry an American girl.''

Now, as I drifted off to sleep, Gene's love and care for me and the boys was assurance enough, I thought, despite guards with bayonets or sound recorders in telephones.

At the end of three weeks I received an invitation from Consul General John Bruins and his wife to visit them in Prague with the children. Papa and Mama were tearful as they bade the grandchildren good-bye. They must have known that we would not be returning, although no word was said. I felt that they were torn between resentment towards a daughter-in-law who would not accept that peace was just around the corner for the country and a nagging fear that our departure was the wiser course.

With Karmazín at the wheel and the boys and I with the nurse bundled in the back, the car rolled through the courtyard and down to the castle gates. I looked back past the urns with their rose-red geraniums to Křižanov, the last time I would ever see it. At the American consulate I thanked Karmazín and he kissed my hand, submissive and inscrutable as ever. Then we were ushered in with cries of welcome by the Bruins.

We lived through a week of patient waiting and exhausting haggling by the government bureaucracy. I stopped asking questions of John Bruins and he volunteered no information. I was sure we would get out of the country. During our wait I had a memorable visit with the Chvalkovskýs. She instructed me to come to the side entrance because they were no longer in their former apartment.

The advice foreshadowed the sad change in their fortunes. Ushered in by a blank-faced butler, I was shocked by the grim expression on the faces of my friends. The Foreign Minister began talking about the tragic events that had occurred in the short time since Gene and I had seen them on our way Paris.

"You will remember how I told you of my daily telephone calls with Herr Hitler. I felt that I could control the situation, however delicate it might be. I truly believed there were boundaries to the Führer's ambitions beyond which it would not serve his purposes to go."

Herr Chvalkovský threw up his hands and his voice became bitter; Hitler's telephone conversations became infrequent; his broadcasts became more belligerent. Then came the day when the Führer refused to accept his call. He had finally written to the German Chargé d'Affaires to request an interview with the Führer for President Hácha. In reply, Hácha and he were commanded to present themselves in the Chancellor's office in Berlin on the afternoon of March 14.

This meant a plane journey in the rough March weather and President Hácha had a heart problem. Chvalkovský gained consent to travel by train and they were met with ceremony in Berlin. Then they had to wait at their hotel throughout the day and until they were summoned into the Führer's presence at 1 a.m. in the night. At the entrance to the Chancellery they were greeted by Foreign Minister Ribbentrop and conducted to the council room. Chvalkovský was startled to see Ribbentrop's ramrod back suddenly slump into a pathetic curve. He looked beyond the general and saw Hitler entering the room.

The Führer led them to a table with a large map of Czechoslovakia on which was recorded the current status of the country – location of ethnic groups, population counts, areas of friction between Germans, Czechs and Slovaks, and the positions of both Czech and German military installations and deployment. Hitler, joined by Goering, pointed out this information to the pale and shaking old president.

"In the best interests of your country," Hitler announced curtly, "Germany will maintain peace and order and will accept Czechoslovakia as a Protectorate under the great German Reich." He then produced a document in which provisions of the Protectorate were set forth in detail and presented it to Hácha to sign.

Hácha, deeply upset, argued that he had no authority to hand over the security of his country; whereupon, Hitler pointed to a telephone and requested him to talk to his Parliament. At this point President Hácha staggered and collapsed to the floor.

Hitler looked startled, said Chvalkovský, and white-faced, called for a doctor, who administered an injection. Hácha revived sufficiently to make the call to Parliament, which had been sitting through the night. Faced with the choice of submission or a devastating invasion, Parliament gave its consent.

The two men returned, but hours before their train reached Prague Hitler's Austrian ground forces had crossed the Czech border. On Hácha's arrival at the Hradshin he found his belongings had been removed from his suite and those of Hitler and his henchmen had been installed.

"The saddest thing for me," said the Foreign Minister, "was the open hostility we now received from my own people. What had been praised as my astute dexterity in handling the Führer was now regarded as my collaboration with him."

I left him and his loyal wife with sadness, and went on to visit Olga Revilliod, daughter of Tomáš Masaryk, who had died a few years earlier. She and her husband received me with open arms and I found them courageous in the midst of tragedy, and with hope for the future. Olga held my hands as I left: "You and Gene will come back, won't you?" I promised, but it was years later in Switzerland that our friendship was renewed.

A few days later my host came in with a great smile and a sheaf of travel tickets in his hand. His smile gave way to a serious expression; "You are going on a visit," said the Consul-General, "and you will offer no explanations, nor draw any attention to your trip." He added that he would arrange for the children's nurse to return to Křižanov. He and Mrs. Bruins saw me quietly on my way next day, with one suitcase, two children and joy in my heart.

As before, however, trouble awaited me at the Czech-German border. When I presented my visa, the German officials went into a huddle, then one of them held out my entry permit. "You have permission to enter, Madam, but I am sorry that your children are not included in the document. They will have to return." He handed me back my papers.

I was astounded and horrified. I studied the permit, while the boys looked ready to break into tears. As I read the words carefully I saw a possible answer to the dilemma. "But it says here that I am permitted to bring in reasonable possessions. Are you telling me that my sons are not my possessions?"

I stared defiantly at the guards, who retreated for further consultation. Soon one of them came and handed me my papers. "You may proceed with your sons, Madam."

With my heart racing and a prayer of thanks on my lips I shepherded the boys back on to the train, and freedom.

An emotional reunion with Gene in Paris, a great send-off by many friends, and we were on our way on a trans-atlantic liner. As we sailed into New York harbor, I stood with Gene, Jerry and Tony at the ship's rail. Never had the Statue of Liberty looked so serene, so full of hope, so warm with welcome. I prayed her lighted torch would shine with wisdom not only for our nation, but for a world in confusion.

We arrived home in San Francisco two weeks before John was born.

11

Desperate Days

DURING THE LONG TRAGIC YEARS of World War II the only word I was able to receive about my family was through the Vatican and the Red Cross. One message came through from each informing me that my parents and my brother were alive. Then, shortly after hostilities in Europe ended, I heard through the Vatican that Mama and Papa were being held in a concentration camp in Jihlava, the county seat of Moravia, and that Mani was in solitary confinement in jail in the county town near Křižanov.

I had been somewhat prepared for this desperate news by Jan Masaryk, when I met him in San Francisco at the founding conference of the United Nations. He was serving as Foreign Minister in the Czech government in exile in London. We talked about the future of his country and at one point he said, ''You and I are friends, but I must tell you we Czechs feel that the only safe German is a dead German. We shall deport the whole German-speaking community.''

At the war's end I heard of terrible bloodshed in Prague as the accumulated hatred between Czechs and the German minority was let loose in atrocities. In addition to that, Russians were transporting Germans in open cattle-cars into the hinterlands of Siberia. Few among the very old and the very young could survive that ordeal. I felt sure that the only hope for my family lay on my shoulders, but all I could do for the moment was to mail CARE packages, hoping they would be received.

At last a letter came from Mani's wife, Alice, from her refuge in Bavaria. She wrote to beg my assistance. She and

Mani had fled before the Russian army, but had been stopped by Czechs at the German-Czech border. The women had been turned loose to make their way through the war-torn German countryside, but the men, including Mani and Alice's brother, had been shipped back to Moravia for 'further questioning.'

She feared that Mani would be brought before a People's Court and condemned to heavy labor, deported and in all probability never be heard from again. She had no idea where he was. Alice had been picked up by an American officer in a jeep as she stumbled alone through the Bavarian woods. Terrified of rape, she had thrown herself on his mercy. He had driven her carefully to a safe haven and left her with a German family. From there she had been able to reach a distant relative who was sustaining her.

For several months I worried and waited, unable to make any move. During the war I had become an American citizen, but no civilians were being permitted into Czechoslovakia unless they had some essential government or business service to perform. I hit on a plan with my brother-in-law, Ed Gallwey, to undertake a commission from him to survey markets for his fruit-dehydration company. The company had furnished large quantities of their products for the military during the war. With these credentials I visited the Czech Ambassador in Washington in April, 1946. He was very dubious about my plans, but after long hours of negotiation I received a visa for unlimited trips to my old country.

Two weeks later, I was on a plane from London to Prague. It was exciting after seven years to hear Czech spoken again and to find Prague remarkably spared from the war damage I saw in many places in the countryside. I drove in a rickety taxi to the Ambassador Hotel and was agreeably surprised by the signs of resurgent prosperity in stores and the city traffic. The resilient Czech spirit, with its determination to get to work, was already creating some order amidst dirt and debris.

I had chosen the Ambassador Hotel as it was reputed to be a meeting ground of foreign business and government bureaucracy. I quickly discovered that as an American who was fluent in Czech I was a welcome guest and the manager installed me in a large room with an impressive bath. My first move was to telephone a man in Jihlava who had been counseling my parents. Dr. Veverka, a well known lawyer, had been the respected mayor. I managed to reach him and told him of my mission. He promised to return my call and after a long delay his reassuring voice came through. He had already obtained permission for my parents to leave their camp to meet me in his office in two days' time.

Exhilarated, I decided to telephone Jan Masaryk, still Minister for Foreign Affairs. His secretary told me Jan was out of town, but would probably be back next day. I resolved to pay him an unannounced visit next morning, but when I arrived at his office in the forbidding old Czernin Palace I was told that Masaryk was still out of town. Dejected, I wandered out through the colonnaded courtyard of the palace to the vast square behind the building. This dead-end square was deserted except for an elderly lady, standing looking lost.

In those days of deep resentments one did not approach strangers and I was veering away from her, to go back into the building. Then an inner murmur drew me back and I asked if I could be of assistance – speaking in Czech. She shook her head. I tried French. No response. Reluctantly I tried German. Then she spoke in English. She was British and had lost her way after visiting a high official in the Ministry. I offered to help her back to her friends, who lived near my hotel. It turned out to be an extremely valuable encounter for me.

We could find no taxi, and on the packed streetcar she began to pour out her tale of failure to rescue her sister, classified as a Sudeten German, from a concentration camp. I quickly stopped her from talking in public and brought her to a quiet corner of my hotel dining room.

There she told me the whole story. She had secured from the Minister of the Interior, Václav Nosek, a leading Communist, what she thought was a strong request for the release of her sister and family. He had added that she would have to get the release signed by the local National Committee of the town in which the family was interned.

"I thought it was a simple matter of red tape," she said, "but when I produced the paper the Committee chairman flatly rejected it, saying his Committee was not about to be dictated to by a government Minister over 'a matter concerning these confounded Germans.' He was adamant. No amount of pleading was of any avail."

My British friend went on to explain that she had learned that the power of these local National Committees was virtually absolute. They had been set up clandestinely during the war to prepare for revolutionary uprisings during the German occupation and for take-over after the liberation. The initiative had come from Czech exiles in Moscow and had been agreed to by the government in exile in London. In most areas Communists had been able to turn the Committees into local "soviets." Late in the war Marshal Malinowsky led his troops through Slovakia, Moravia and into Bohemia, not only liberating their fellow Slavs, but systematically strengthening these National Committees.

As I listened to this discouraged lady I became thoroughly shaken. I realized how close I had come to making exactly the same mistake. I must rethink my strategy – forget Masaryk and begin in Moravia. Before she left, the lady and I made a pact we would help one another by sharing information and useful contacts.

As I made my way to Dr. Veverka two days later, I knew my next move must be to get to Velké Meziříčí, where brother Mani was interned in the county prison. And eventually, I now understood, I would have to go to Křižanov to plead the cause of all three of my family. As I made the four-hour train trip to meet my parents I felt weighed down by all the difficulties. Gradually, as I gazed out at the familiar countryside, fresh and beautiful in the May sunshine, my spirits rose. This was the time of year I used to go out in the evenings to stalk roebuck or wait for the flight of the woodcock in the woods and meadows of our place. The game, I felt sure, was still there, and peasants were still out, bending to sow the spring seed.

My fellow passengers were discussing the elections, only two weeks away, and everyone seemed to realize their importance. As they talked, it was clear that they looked forward to democracy – but what kind? The American pattern, championed by their beloved Tomáš Masaryk, or the Russian type of "People's Democracy"? I was fascinated to listen to their serious arguing, but when they discovered that I was an American they wanted to draw me out on my views. One of them said Masaryk and Wilson were still great heroes in their land.

"Tell us," one asked, "is America going to stay friends with Russia? Are we going to be able to keep our traditional friendship with you, or are you in the West going to abandon us the way you did at Munich?"

As I fumbled for an answer, feeling the pain I always did when that subject came up, a vocal young peasant spoke up: "I am a Communist now. I fought in the underground during the war and now I'm chairman of our National Committee. If you want my honest opinion, I'll tell you I would honestly prefer the American kind of democracy. But we are so close to Russia and their power is growing, so I believe their People's Democracy is the coming thing. And that's what I've chosen. You can't stop it."

I looked at the faces around me; they seemed to register consternation, fear, rebellion, but no one responded to the young man. I had the feeling that the Czech in these times was cautious about expressing his convictions about the Soviets in a public place.

Dr. Veverka was waiting for me at the station. As we made our way to his office I thanked him most warmly for taking on the legal representation of my parents and brother. Not only was there little hope of adequate remuneration, but it had taken great courage to represent three former members of the Sudeten German Party before the authorities and the People's Court. During the war he had shown an equal sense of justice when he placed all his prestige on the line in defending his Czech countrymen against the Gestapo. He told me that the post-war turn of events had impacted more than three million German- and Hungarian-speaking citizens who lived within the borders of Bohemia, Moravia, Silesia and Slovakia. He well understood why it had come about, but he deplored the cruel situations it produced. He was helping Papa, he said, because he had admired and respected him for years.

Mama and Papa were not due to come to his office until the next morning and I was glad to be able to talk first with this wise lawyer about their situation and Mani's. So, that evening we talked far into the night at the Veverka apartment where he'd invited me to stay with him and two maiden sisters. He told me of my family's determination to remain in the country. They wanted to vindicate their loyalty to their native land.

"Believe me," he said, "the situation here is so volatile that no one can count on anyone in the German minority receiving justice. Our people have suffered too much, and the pent-up hatred is being used by the Communists through their People's Courts."

Veverka added that he understood my parents' deep love of the land, and how hard it would be for them to accept the situation, but he believed that if I could possibly succeed in getting them out of the country that was what I must do.

Early next morning I awoke torn by two emotions, excitement at seeing my parents again after so long, and concern as to whether I could rescue them from their world of hardship and desperation. To prepare myself for the day I spent time in meditation and then went to early Mass and Communion in a nearby church.

At ten o'clock, punctual as ever, Papa and Mama stepped into Veverka's office. For several minutes we could only hug each other tightly, choked with our feelings too deep for expression. Then I held them at arm's length. They were very thin, but looked surprisingly well. Papa, with his 78 years and Mama at 70 both stood erect. Dressed in very old and patched clothes, they still looked a noble pair. Only after a while did I notice that each had a white band around the left arm. When I asked about it they told me that all Sudeten Germans were obliged to wear this sign of inferiority and contempt which the Nazis had earlier imposed on the Jews.

For the next three hours much of our talk with Veverka was spent in a factual discussion of their situation, with the lawyer giving thoughtful advice on what must be done. Yet the tragic story of their past years poured out from them in fragments. When the victorious Russian army arrived in Křižanov Papa and Mama had fled in fear into the woods to the home of their most loyal forester at Sichy. There he had hidden them in his cellar, fed them and reassured them as best he could. But within hours a detachment of Russian soldiers came clattering down the stairs and hauled them out.

To their horror they were told that their trusted Karmazín, not just a chauffeur, but for years a trusted member of the family circle, had tipped off the soldiers as to their whereabouts. Later they learned that he had been for some years the ranking under-cover Communist of the region. Papa and Mama were prodded outside with bayonets and forced to stand with their faces to the wall. If they moved a muscle, they were told, they would be shot.

They were given fifteen minutes to live. At the end of that time they were granted a further fifteen minutes. For one quarter hour after another they were submitted to this torture. Finally, after sixteen hours the old couple were allowed to drop exhausted to the ground and were then herded back into the cellar. The forester was threatened with execution if he let them out.

After a cold and hungry night the soldiers returned with Karmazín and another local Communist. Their first command was, "Tell us where your jewelry is hidden." Karmazín, a trusted member of the household staff, knew about all their possessions. Papa stated firmly that they had long ago sent all their jewelry out of the country. This provoked a violent reaction from the two men, who shouted, kicked them and then forced them outside, where a cattle truck waited. Mama had often coddled Karmazín, even personally nursing him through his stomach attacks. She was unable now to contain her shock at this young man's betrayal and burst into bitter tears.

Then, when the other Communist went into the house, Karmazín ran to my mother and whispered, "Your Grace, please forgive me. I hope you will understand that I have to do this to you. This is nothing against you personally, but the old order has to go, and you happen to be part of it." Karmazín looked tragic and bent to kiss Mama's hand. At that moment the other Communist came out of the house and Karmazín straightened up, gave her a brutal kick and told her with an oath to crawl up into the truck.

My parents were taken to their first camp in the county seat of Velké Meziříčí. On the way they passed a herd of Papa's prize Bernese cattle being driven for slaughter for the Russian army. In this camp they were crowded in with other landowners, industrialists and such-like "bourgeois German swine" under appalling conditions. The women and men were separated and all were housed in barracks, nearly a score to a small vermin-ridden room, with minimal sleeping and sanitary facilities. For weeks on end their food consisted of pieces of bread, ersatz coffee and watery potato soup. Each lost fifty to sixty pounds in less than three months. Mama had two teeth knocked out by a guard in a fit of temper.

"Every morning," Mama related, "we lined up in the courtyard for work, men on one side, women on the other.

That was the only time I was able to see your father. Then the Russian guards would each select their work gang. The younger women trembled at this point for fear that their guard would misuse them. I remember one morning especially. The sun was rising, casting a deep red glow through the courtyard entrance and silhouetted at the top of the stairs stood a huge brute of a guard, swinging his *nagajka* (a whip with strips of leather in which were knotted pieces of iron.) He looked like the devil incarnate, with hell fire behind him, as he eyed his victims below.

"At that moment I promised God that if I ever should get out from under this monster, I would give myself to Him as completely as I was now in the power of this devil. And I still mean what I promised then."

Mama's drawn face had a glimmer of a smile. She went on to talk as I'd never heard her talk before. "There was hatred and bitterness burning in me during those long nights, but more than that there was the terrible fear I would never see you again, Genus. I wanted to tell you how wrong we'd been about your inheritance."

She looked at Papa and he nodded. I said gently, "Mama, that's all in the past," and patted her hand. But she wanted to finish her story. One night, she said, she began to think about what one old woman might still do in that horrible place. Next morning, when the two surly guards called her to work at five o'clock to sweep the streets in the village, she had decided she would do the job perfectly. She worked quietly and well all that morning and suddenly, when she looked at the guards, she thought, they're only children, not more than sixteen years old. She must have stared at those two clods, she said, because she saw they were gazing back at her in a perplexed way. She must have smiled a little, because a grin appeared on their faces. A very small thing, and yet it had been the start of happier days in the camp, and she knew in her heart that she would see me again.

Mama got up and put her arms around me, holding me

tight. Veverka stepped out of the room and came back shortly with cool drinks for us all. Then Papa picked up the tale, describing how he had worked ten hours a day, every day, carrying bricks from war ruins for a new building. At their age and on a diet of potato soup, this was a life and death test of ability to survive. And their desperation had taught them to draw on hitherto untouched depths of faith and determination.

"It was strange," said Father. "We'd lost everything and yet gained something new – you might call it a sense of responsibility for those around us that helped us stand up, for their sakes as well as our own."

Then one day, Papa went on, a miracle had happened. A delegation arrived unexpectedly from their village, a citizen's committee with a request for the release of the aged couple and an offer of care for them in Křižanov in one of the small huts used for the poor. These citizens, it seemed, had obtained permission from the all-powerful local National Committee on which Karmazín had now become the controlling influence. The camp commander in Velké Meziříčí had been only too glad to get rid of two mouths belonging to two not-very-useful old people.

So they arrived at the little house in the village beneath their castle. From this hut they could watch the daily dismantling and wanton breaking of furniture in their old home. Papa, too, could see his fields and model farming installations slowly going to ruin – the ruin of all he had built during his adult life.

At the same time, he said, they were both deeply moved by the many kindnesses villagers showed. Indeed, even some who were rabid Communists by day came secretly by night to bring food, cigarettes and even money. After Mass on Sunday some folk would unobtrusively sidle up to them to slip a banknote or coin into their pockets. One day an old villager had arrived with Mama's pet spaniel, Neggy, for which he had cared. He had put up a fight before the People's Committee to obtain permission, and now stood beaming with Neggy in his arms.

"If ever we get back any of our possessions," said Papa, "I would like to do something to show my gratitude for all those favors from all kinds of people. They each took a chance on being called traitors; they even risked their freedom – and they had nothing to gain from us."

It was from that hut that they had written to me, enabling Dorothy and me to send them CARE packages. In their letters they had expressed their trust that their "American son" could accomplish what no one else could do. And as we sat here together now it was borne in on me that it was this hope more than anything else that had sustained them through the years. God help me to be adequate!

After a few months in the village hut they had received an order to move to another camp within three days. They were told that Schloss Námněšť, which belonged to our great friends and distant relatives, Graf Heinrich Haugwitz and his wife Alice, had been offered by Moravia as a summer seat for the President of the Republic. As a precautionary measure, all "democratically and ideologically unreliable" elements in a radius of twenty miles must be removed. That included Papa and Mama. They also heard that 150 pounds of new and heirloom silver that they had hidden, and that had been quickly discovered, was now to be shipped to Namiest.

Once again a big truck carted them away, together with a few other old people, to this camp in Jihlava. It was a sad departure from Křižanov, where they had met with kindness. Worse than that, they knew that the camp might well afford only a temporary respite in their wanderings. Many people, old and young, were still being deported to Siberia.

Quietly, Dr. Veverka broke into Mama's reminiscences to suggest that it was time to come to grips with all the practical legal and other issues involved in the release of my parents. He cautiously broached the question of our basic purpose – to find a secure haven for Papa and Mama. He stressed that the only safe course was to plan wisely for their voluntary emigration, first probably to Switzerland. I held my breath, knowing of Papa's past determination to remain in this country. To my surprise and relief he agreed at once that this was the sensible course.

We launched into a discussion of the almost insurmountable legal difficulties in obtaining permission, first to leave the camp, then to leave the country, and finally to establish a right to citizenship that would enable them to live abroad. Then we realized that the allotted three hours for my parents' visit was at an end. Mama, with a little smile, invited me to lunch with them. Knowing how limited was their supply of food, I hesitated, but she said they had some delicacies all ready.

"The Camp commander has agreed to let you come in for lunch and the afternoon," she said. "After all, you are an American and he wants to meet you and talk with you about democracy in America. Also, Papa has built up a certain position for us in the camp. Come on, we'll make it a celebration!"

"What a pair!," I thought, as I stepped out with them to walk the two miles to the camp. I was horrified to see my parents step off the sidewalk and start walking on the narrow street amidst the crowded traffic of automobiles, trucks and bicycles, but when I started to draw them back on to the sidewalk they stopped me. Papa pointed to his white arm band and whispered, "We are not allowed to walk on the sidewalk. Please just walk alongside us without any fuss, so we don't attract attention. Further on we can take a back alley without sidewalks."

At the entrance to the camp a guard took us directly to the Commander. He seemed pleased to meet me. I noticed that he addressed Papa respectfully and when I spoke in Czech he beamed, offered us seats and said I was welcome at the camp at any time. "I hope, Sir Doctor," he added, "that you may find the time to tell me something of America."

Despite what they had told me I was shocked when my

parents led me into their room. It was some eight by twelve feet, with bunk beds, two rickety chairs and a board fastened to the window sill to serve as a table. Very little light came through the small window covered with a heavy iron grill. Yet the place was spic-and-span.

Mama went off to get three portions of soup and some bread from the communal kitchen – the extra ration for me was thanks to the sharing of some of the camp inmates. Then she brought out from under a bunk some treasures saved up for this feast. Over an alcohol burner she cooked some meat from a can, a chocolate pudding, followed by coffee. This had all been saved from our CARE packages, some of which they had shared with people in special need of strengthening food.

Over our festive meal I remarked on their generosity to fellow prisoners. That drew some surprising philosophy from Papa: "You know, Genus, times like these show up the qualities in people. There are those who live only in the past, full of bitterness and despair. That's sad, because they miss the satisfaction of doing things for others and as a result become increasingly mean and frightened."

On the other hand, he went on, character and conviction showed up dramatically in others. For example, those who had come to visit them and then to get them out of the camp in Velké Meziříčí were real heroes. That city had been the scene of a last stand by the Nazis, during which they had murdered a score of young Czechs whom they suspected of underground activities. Imagine the hatred they left in that town towards Germans. He and Mama encountered it when they were taken on forced marches through its streets – they were spat upon, kicked and hit. So it was into that atmosphere that people from Křižanov came, first to visit them and then to plead for their transfer to Křižanov.

"It must have been a joy," I said, "to get back to our village."

Mama put a hand on my arm. "Genus, of course it was at first, but those months in Křižanov became in many ways the hardest to bear. To see the beauty that I had created in the castle being systematically demolished! And Papa had to watch his fields, his game, his ponds being deliberately allowed to wither away. For a while it took all hope out of us.''

Her voice rose sharply and tears spilled down her face. ''No, strange as it may seem, we were glad to come here, away from all we had known and loved.''

Papa reached out to hold her hand. ''Your Mother and I had been through the destruction of the First World War and I kept thinking for a while that we would be able to rebuild again like last time. But, you know, matters are turning out very differently. There are forces at work which want to obliterate everything we stood for.'' He paused and looked at me. ''Genus, we can't go back. We've got to move forward.''

Mama said, ''That's true. And we've got to live differently. My concerns used to be all inside myself, but I'm not nearly so obstreperous as I used to be, am I, Eugene?'' She laughed and added, ''Papa upholds me, too. With his wisdom and courage he gives balance to us all.''

I looked at the two of them in this bare little room and I pictured them back in the magnificence of Schloss Křižanov. I marvelled at them now, talking about happiness, friendship, kindness and courage. Their world had become small and grim, but their spirit had grown a thousand-fold.

Gently I began asking news about some of our relatives. What about Uncle Carl and Aunt Biba?

''When Carl learned that the Russian troops were coming close,'' said Mama, ''he took Biba out into the birch forest they both loved so dearly, and they started to walk. Her heart was very frail and they both knew that she would never be able to withstand the treatment she could expect from the Russians. They walked until she failed. Carl held her in his arms until she died and then he buried her there. It was what she wanted and it was the better way. Carl was sent to a concentration camp and as far as we know, he's still there."

Mama went on to tell about her sister Mizi, with whom she had been very close. She had married a Count and our family was very fond of them both. She broke into tears as she said, "Mizi couldn't get away before the Russian soldiers broke into their home. They went up to her room and . . ." She broke down, then went on painfully, "When they left her . . . she jumped out of the window to her death."

"Genus," she said timidly as I put my arms around her, "Do you think God would call that suicide?"

I told her from the depths of my heart that I was sure we could trust Aunt Mizi to Him.

There was so much to talk about, but now I must leave, because visiting time was up; a guard arrived to remind me. We still chatted on, and he came back to order me to leave immediately, or I would not be permitted to return. I said a quick farewell and started to rush across the courtyard to the gate.

Suddenly I heard Papa call in his familiar voice of authority, "My boy, please come back!"

I automatically hurried back to him. He said quietly, but firmly, "My son, please realize I have built a certain position of respect for your Mother and myself in this camp and I do not wish you to undermine it by showing an undue sense of hurry."

As I walked slowly towards the gate I thought to myself, "Not bad – for the inmate of a concentration camp who has lost everything but his own self-esteem."

12

Legal Dilemma

SATISFIED that we had made a good start in the battle for the release of Papa and Mama, next day I embarked on what Dr. Veverka had told me would be the even tougher task of prying my brother loose from his prison. Veverka said that Mani's case was very difficult because it had to be pleaded before a Special People's Court on which only one member was a lawyer; the rest had no legal knowledge.

I took the two-hour train ride with Veverka to the county prison in Velké Meříčí. The jail was housed in the county building and when we asked the warden for directions to Mani's cell he told us that through good behavior Mani had been given permission to work half-days in the county office. The warden looked at me with curiosity and asked if I was Mani's American brother. When I admitted that I was, he bowed obsequiously and led us himself to the large room that housed the county archives.

Standing in the doorway I looked across tables piled high with books and papers to the far end of the room, where I saw my brother bent over his work. Then he heard us and straightened up. I will never forget the waves of emotion crossing his face – amazement, unbelief, shock, joy. Then he ran towards me and threw his arms around me,nearly choking me as he shook with convulsive sobs.

I knew Mani to be a courageous man, but a year in solitary confinement, with constant threats of deportation to the oblivion of the uranium mines, had sapped his spirit. On top of that, he had received no news of his wife Alice since he had seen her forced to trudge into the German forests. I stood quietly, my own heart too full for words, while his

130

Tomáš Masaryk (second from right) with son Jan and family in the garden
of Castle Lány

Gene, Dorothy and Mani with friends listening to the daily news broadcast
in the tense period just before Hitler's take-over of Czechoslovakia

Gene, Dorothy and their sons, Jerry, Tony and John in their San Francisco home

Baron Eugene and Countess Anna von Teuber in Geneva following their escape

Schloss Gandegg in the Italian Tyrol where the senior von Teubers spent their later years

Mani and Alice in the garden of their new home in Germany

Schloss Křižanov as it appears today. Pictured left to right: The Mayor of Křižanov, the director of the Children's Center, Jerry von Teuber and friend

Schloss chapel as restored by the Parish Pastor

Village of Křižanov today

tears coursed down his face. Then slowly I began to reassure him; I repeated over and over that Alice was safe, that we would take care of her, and that we would take care of him and Papa and Mama as well. He couldn't seem to grasp all my words, but they calmed him and soon he was coherent enough to ask questions.

After giving him the highlights of news of all the family I told him with all the confidence I could muster of the plans Veverka and I had concocted in the past couple of days. I knew he was coming to life when a big grin appeared and he said, "You poor hungry fellow, I must feed you! I have more than enough – wait, I'll have tea served immediately!"

I was startled; I hadn't yet realized just what a large part food played in the thoughts of prison inmates. He had me laughing as he clapped his hands for service with mock authority and said, "Putze, I can never seem to find the servants around here, although everything else is taken care of – no worries about the weather, choice of clothes or anything. All is provided!

"Seriously, though, it's been touching the way people from Křižanov and other villages around here have been taking care of me. I get so many things. Lard and meat, even butter and cake – unimaginable delicacies they bring me." He added slyly, "Of course I pass a lot of them on to others, otherwise I'd get too fat and satisfied and stay here forever!"

At this point, Dr. Veverka, who had remained discreetly in the background, came forward and Mani greeted him warmly. "Here is the man," he said to me, with a touch of desperation in his voice, "who is surely going to get me out of here."

We walked to a corner where we could sit amidst the array of papers, and I asked, "Who are these people, Mani, who are giving you these gifts, and how do they get permission to see you?"

"It's mostly people I helped during the war. I fought for them with the German authorities, and in some cases I think

I saved their lives. Some of them are Communists. They come at night and the guards let them in because they know I'll share my food with them too. And some of the guards are scared of the Communists.''

Then he took us to see his store of food supplies. I was amazed and told my brother it was abundant evidence of his courageous role during the war. This brought a torrent of words from Mani: ''Well, we must plan how we can get all these people to help vindicate me of all the absurd accusations held against me so I can get out of here. I've already begun to collect affidavits from people who will testify that I saved their lives during the war. Why, I even used to go to Gestapo headquarters to fight for these people. They will certainly stand up for me before the People's Court.''

Mani turned to Veverka and his voice was rising excitedly: ''Doctor, I've already managed to collect half a dozen of these affidavits and I've been promised another thirty or so. Surely that's going to establish my innocence, isn't it, and get me out of this place and off to join my wife?''

Dr. Veverka answered him in a hushed voice, often glancing around to make sure no one could overhear him. ''Please don't assume that you will receive a fair judgment from the People's Court. You may, but you can't rely on it, especially in this hate-filled atmosphere of Velké Meziříčí. Now, I know the one man on the Court who is a jurist. He's a decent fellow and I'll get his advice on the best approach.'' He turned to me: ''I would like to introduce you to him. He's a great admirer of the United States.''

Mani objected. He reiterated forcefully that he must be vindicated and felt his case was powerful and he must fight it through. Veverka shook his head and repeated politely but firmly that it would be a great mistake to rely on the impartiality of the Court. He asked to see the affidavits Mani had collected.

They were full of praise, very touching in their expressions of gratitude. One in particular has stayed in my mind; a young man we used to regard as the village rowdy, now a Communist and on the Křižanov National Committee, wrote that "citizen Teuber" had saved his life and the lives of many others through intervention with the Nazis. However, the letter also made it blatantly evident that Mani, out of the goodness of his heart, while listening to the pleadings of our village elders for mercy following the German occupation at the start of the war, had accepted a position in the Nazi regime.

I had been told by Veverka that in order to better defend villagers Mani had become a *Blockleiter* for Křižanov. At the time Alice had pleaded in tears that he refuse the position, but he had felt that by taking on this lowest rank in the Nazi hierarchy he could carry out his "inborn duty to protect his people," and that if he refused it, his people would be penalized.

Therefore, however humanitarian his motives, Mani was now saddled with the ugly fact of his identification with Nazidom. This was a murderous weapon in the hands of anyone who now wanted to destroy him. As I listened to my brother and the lawyer weighing the pros and cons I became increasingly disturbed. I could see with some objectivity that a more powerful approach was needed in this hate-filled area than a mere presentation of the facts of the case. Somehow I must find a way to win people rather than just trying to win a legal case.

I turned to Veverka. "Do you think you could reach your lawyer friend on the Court right now?"

"Yes," said Veverka thoughtfully, "you are right. That is the next move. I will try to reach him."

Mani was disappointed by our decision. He had placed great hopes in a dramatic justification before the Court. As Veverka went off, I set out to explain to my brother why I felt that the key lay in winning the hearts and minds of individuals on the Court, rather than just producing brilliant arguments or even powerful evidence. I told him how much raw emotion I had encountered on my return to Czechoslovakia, how so many were still in the grip of the cruel past. It was imperative to build bridges of trust once again, opening hearts as well as appealing to intellects.

Mani responded by getting up and going to his food cupboard. "This is *gemütlich*," he said, "and deserves a feast!" This was the highest approbation from a Moravian Austrian. He beckoned to a fellow prisoner and to a prison guard to join us, and we attacked cakes and cookies in a jovial celebration.

We were suddenly recalled from our cheerful partying by the arrival of a burly jailer, clanging his keys and stepping in to remove Mani firmly to his cell. I asked him if I might see the place where my brother had spent these last long months alone. He hesitated, then agreed and led us to a heavy door at the entrance to the prison wing. He was about to step through ahead of us, then stopped, stepped back, bowed to me and motioned for us to go ahead.

"After you," I said.

"Oh, no, Sir Baron, please go ahead." Then, turning to Mani, he added, "And you also, Sir Baron."

Then he suddenly seemed to recollect himself, growled some inaudible order and followed us. I smiled to myself at the irony of a feudal past that still intruded on a revolutionary present.

Mani's cell was all that I had imagined it to be − a hard bunk, the inevitable small, high, screened window letting in a minimum of light. A quick embrace, and the door closed between us.

Dr. Veverka was waiting outside to take me to the lawyer who sat on the People's Court. "He's looking forward to meeting you − I think he wants to show off his English!"

On entering the man's office I was struck by his honest looks and his cordial greeting. I answered him in Czech and then added a few words in slow, careful English. His face lit up and soon we were launched into an animated conversation on the merits of democracy, especially the American variety. He said frankly that he wanted to use his position to further the best interests of justice in the somewhat chaotic post-war society. He counted on Czechoslovakia's continued friendship with the United States.

At one point he said his greatest wish was to learn good English, largely, I gathered, in order to advance his interests in common law and international law. On an impulse I offered to give him some lessons and to procure for him the right text books from Prague. His face lit up. He was clearly surprised, but accepted with alacrity. We arranged on the spot that during my stay in Moravia I would come to Velké Meziříčí once or twice a week to give him lessons.

Before returning to Jihlava I decided to pay a visit to Louis and Jozy Podstadsky-Lichtenstein. Count and Countess Podstadsky were old friends and among our closest neighbors when we lived in Křižanov. Jozy was a cousin of Alice Teuber. I had heard that Louis had worked with the Czech underground resistance during the German occupation and had actually joined the *Partisani* fighters during the last days of the war. He was therefore regarded as something of a hero by Czechs and it was for this reason that the family still retained their beautiful hilltop castle. On the other hand, their extensive wealth and Austrian aristocratic background placed them at a severe disadvantage. I was therefore not only eager to renew our friendship but also to learn how secure was their present status. This was my first opportunity, too, to visit my Austrian-Czech compatriots outside prison walls.

I walked up a steep hill above the city and stood in front of the great gate in the battlements. Facing me was a large poster attached to the iron knobs of the old iron door. It announced in Czech and Russian: "A National Monument protected by the State." As I walked into the courtyard nothing seemed to have changed; the great old coat of arms still hung on the wall above the main portal. The stables, garages, cars were still there; a spreading centuries-old tree still shadowed the yard.

A servant in a somewhat shabby livery was crossing the

courtyard and I stopped him. He recognized me, but refused to look me in the eye. I asked where his "masters" were in the castle — one did not ask for "Count" or "Countess" any more. He replied sulkily that "citizens Podstadsky" were at home, then reverting suddenly to more courteous ways, he went ahead and bowed while opening the door that led to the grand staircase. I went through one drawing room after another and finally reached a smaller, more cozy room where I found the whole family — father, mother and three teenaged children at tea.

It seemed at first as though time had stood still. Jozy was pouring fragrant tea from a silver pot, but as I walked through the door there was a moment of frozen fear on their faces. Then, stunned but joyous, they embraced me with kisses and I was sat down and bombarded with cakes and questions. How did I get there? Where had I been? What was I doing? Then more wide flung queries — what did the Americans, the English, the French, think of what was going on here?

I noticed that all the questions were discreetly framed; no one asked about Mama and Papa, and the conversation was all in Czech and English, none in German. Jozy asked carefully about Alice — "I hear she is with . . . friends. Leaving the country must have been hard for her?" I told her Alice was well but very uncertain about her future. I saw a tear trickling down Jozy's cheek.

They were all obviously aware of the servants, who were coming and going during our conversation. At one moment when they were all out of the room Louis whispered to me, "Please watch everything you say, Putze, in front of the servants. They all report on us and one is a local leader of the Communist Party."

So our hour's conversation before I had to leave to catch the train back to Jihlava was limited to talk of the Partisans, the last days of the war and the victories of the Allies, especially of "the great Soviet armies."

I could read the sadness in Louis' eyes when he spoke

of Marshal Rodien Malinowsky's troops who had "liberated" this part of Moravia. At one point he looked at me with a perfectly blank expression and said, "Yes, the Government has honored us with the sign you saw plastered on the gate. It makes the property sacrosanct from requisition by any Czech or Russian."

When time came to leave they begged me to stay and then insisted on having me driven to my train. I promised to return for a longer visit. As the car took me through the gates I mused on the differing fates of this family and of my own. Louis and Jozy live on in their estate; Papa and Mama were in a detention camp – but both couples were prisoners.

13

Inspired Strategy

ON THE TRAIN back to Jihlava, Veverka and I studied the affidavits Mani had handed to us and found they bore witness to no less than 48 persons my brother had saved from execution by the Nazis. The lawyer agreed that this was powerful evidence. Veverka was even more happy about the friendship I appeared to have struck up with the jurist member of the Court. "Your offer to give him English lessons was inspired," he said.

I laughed. "You labeled it correctly. It was 'inspiration.' I can't claim it as my own genius at work. You know, Doctor, these days I find myself constantly beyond my depth, and I spend longer time in prayer and meditation."

Veverka gave me a sidelong look. "I've been watching you at work and I've wondered how you often come up with apt solutions that often seem trivial at the moment. To be honest, God and the Church have been little more than venerable institutions for me, scarcely relevant to the revolutionary times in which we're living."

"Well," I agreed, "faith is a much misused word. But perhaps it gives us a dimension we need, especially in the chaos man is producing. I believe it strengthens the discipline we need in order to contribute towards order and peace."

Veverka admitted that something more solid was needed on which to build a decent world. He had put his trust in Beneš and his political strategy, but clearly human wisdom and humanitarian principles were insufficient. We fell silent and I knew he was pursuing in his methodical mind this new avenue of thought.

138

Next day was taken up with the preparation of legal papers and petitions – each had to be couched in the exact language and bear the correct stamp. At one point Veverka clapped me on the shoulder and said with a smile, "All this paraphernalia is fine and I'll put the papers in your hands, but you'd better accompany them with that 'higher wisdom' of yours – you're going to need it!"

Then he became very serious as he went on to talk about Mani's situation. Only one in a thousand of the ethnic Germans and Austrians who were being processed for deportation received permission instead to emigrate elsewhere. We were attempting the almost impossible for my parents, and even more so for Mani. He said he must make the attempt, however, because if my parents went away on one of those deportation trains, they would probably never arrive alive at their destination.

"The same is true of course of your brother," he added. "The accusations he faces could legally condemn him to five to ten years forced labor in the uranium mines. You would never hear from him again. This sounds brutal, but it's wiser to face the cold facts now."

I knew what he was talking about. I had heard from others descriptions of the open cattle-cars, which were sent to the Soviet or Northern Germany, sometimes all the way to Siberia, with almost no food provided for a stretch of a week or more, and no sanitary facilities beyond a hole in the floor.

There was another reason to worry about Mani's fate. I had been told that some of his accusers were motivated by the fear that should he be vindicated they might lose to him or to me property they had gained from our family.

The lawyer and I mapped out my strategy, which involved not only the presentation of these papers in due course before the People's Court but, equally vital, my pleading the cases before the local National Committee in Křižanov. Clearly I would have to do a lot of traveling between here, Velké Meziříčí, Křižanov and Prague. That afternoon I started my journeys with a return to Prague to have the petitions stamped by the correct Government departments.

My state of mind was not improved by posters newly plastered on the streets and at the railway stations in preparation for national elections to be held in a few days. The majority of the signs were Communist propaganda attacking ''the bourgeois classes'' and also against Germans and collaborators – not a healthy environment for Mani or my parents. At one point we rolled slowly past one of those deportation trains standing on a siding. People stared at us with hate-filled faces; some shook their fists and yelled at us.   I began to feel intensely depressed. My mission seemed just too futile, hedged about with cruelty on one side and complacency on the other. Then, as I thought about how the way had opened up for me so far, and how difficult people had responded to a positive spirit, I took heart again.

Back at the Ambassador Hotel I was received as an old friend and next morning set off into the lion's den, the Ministry of the Interior, armed with a packet of petitions, all in triplicate.

At the first office, recommended by Veverka, I was gruffly rebuffed and sent on to a second office. There I was able to produce documents attesting to my having worked effectively in the cause of industrial teamwork to improve productivity for the Allies in World War II. All to no avail.

I was handed on from one office to another. It became obvious to me that Václav Nosek, Minister of the Interior, had accomplished a very thorough job in filling his Ministry with loyal Communists. After several hours of rebuff and filling out pointless forms I decided to leave and head for the American Embassy.

My good friend John Bruins was now serving there as First Secretary and right-hand man to Ambassador Steinhard and he welcomed me warmly. As I told him about my mission and the roadblocks I had encountered I found he, like others I had met in our diplomatic service, was naive about the degree of ideological penetration of governments with whom we had been allies in wartime. He still clung to the hope that the United States and our Western allies could continue our honeymoon of cooperation with the Soviet Union. He added that it was largely for this reason that his Embassy had not intervened in cases in which Sudeten Germans were involved, even though it was aware of some gross injustices being perpetrated. Any such intervention, he felt, could jeopardize American support for democratic forces in Czechoslovakia. Under these circumstances he deeply regretted that he could not help me.

Bruin's advice to me was to call on the Embassy's lawyer, whose standing with the Czech authorities was high. I went directly to his office and found the gentleman cooperative. He helped rephrase several of the petitions. Then we found ourselves in a lengthy discussion of the political and ideological state of the country. He was aware of the dangers, but optimistic about the future and even suggested that as an American citizen I should initiate legal proceedings for return of our estates or for due compensation.

"But don't for Heaven's sake," he added, "breathe a word about such an idea until you have your parents and your brother safely out of the country!" He went on to tell me that the Minister of Agriculture was also a Communist, and should he ever get wind of such an action, would have the Křižanov local National Committee make violent accusations against my family, with the result that they would be sent to a maximum security prison and all our lands would at once be confiscated. "His Ministry plans on parceling out your property to each man who votes Communist."

We went on to talk about the prospects for my petition to the Ministry of Agriculture. "I tell you what you do," he said. "Give a package of cigarettes to the man to whom you turn in your petition, and suggest that there may be more of the same when you return to pick up the processed document."

I had been told by others that this was the customary procedure, and in the case of a high official a large sum of money was necessary. I had answered that I did not have large sums of money, nor was I disposed to offer bribes. However, I did just as the legal officer had suggested, and it worked out as he had said it would.

Back in my hotel room, however, I faced a hard decision. At the start of my mission over here I had resolved not to give bribes. This had seemed such a minor one, and I knew that most people would have regarded any scruples about it as naive stupidity. But my conscience wouldn't be appeased and next day I returned to the official and apologized for the dishonor I had done him and his government by making use of American cigarettes as a weapon.

The poor man understandably looked stunned, but he thanked me with an embarrassed smile and soon we found ourselves launched into a discussion of the future as two democrats, Czech and American. I heard from him the same theme many others had told me: he believed in the American way, but under the present circumstances he felt it was wiser to choose the Russian style.

I left with the conviction that time was not on my side. There were still many Czechs like him who clung to the memory of America and Russia as allies in the liberation of their country, but that conviction was being fast eroded.

While in Prague I was using every opportunity to meet with people I had known and trusted who might give me valuable confidential information about the national situation. I invited to dinner at the hotel a cousin, Cary and his beautiful wife. He was a bright, charming, well educated young businessman, son of a landowner baron and related by marrige to several families who, before the war, controlled part of Czechoslovakia's economic life. But with his family background he was well aware of his limited prospects; later they emigrated to Canada.

In a quiet corner of the restaurant he talked about the last hectic days of the war, when such violent bloodshed took place on the streets of Prague. As the German Wehrmacht was being forced to leave the city the Russian-trained Czech partisans were encouraged by the Soviets to attack the retreating soldiers. The German High Command ordered troops back into Prague to protect their rearguard and as a result, on May 6, 1945, there occurred a massacre of more than two thousand Czechs at the barricades. This was followed in turn by days and weeks of savage atrocities inflicted on German civilians and German-speaking Czechs in Prague.

The Communists were quick to spread the rumor that the American military had been deliberately held back from battle in order to protect their forces. Cary told me indignantly that emissaries from Czech President Hácha had been sent to the American military, waiting on the Pilsen-Karlsbad line, begging them to advance on Prague. They had not responded.

"Why in the name of sanity did you Americans not come and liberate Prague?" asked Cary. "They could have saved all that terrible bloodshed. I suppose you all did not realize the opportunity you missed, or maybe your troops faltered at that moment."

Knowing the caliber of General Patton, commander of those troops, I quickly disabused Cary of that idea. I told him the sad fact was that Stalin and Roosevelt at Teheran and again at Yalta had made their compact that our forces would halt where they did. It was Stalin, and his Czech Communist colleagues, who were responsible for that Prague tragedy.

Cary stared at me in confusion. "I came within a millimeter of losing my life during those days," he said. "I was walking along a narrow street when I ran into a mob out for revenge. Someone had seized two steam rollers and they were being driven down a blind alley to crush the men, women and children ahead of them. Someone saw me and yelled, 'There's another damned aristocrat!' Fortunately for me a Czech, who recognized me, saved me. The rest were crushed in that dead-end street."

My young cousin was now so wound up he kept on relating horror stories he had himself witnessed – people burned at the stake, torn to pieces. I would have liked to stop him but realized he had to express his rage to someone who would not react as his Czech friends would have done. His wife sat white-faced and trembling and I turned to her and started asking about their marriage and future plans.

Slowly Cary subsided and we were able to talk together quietly about past, present and future. They were both good friends of Mani and conversation led to details of my mission, my rounds of the government ministries and even to my bribe with the cigarettes and my retraction.

"You certainly risked burning your bridges behind you that time," Cary exclaimed. "But I think I understand why you did it. You have a faith, and faith has a price. Well God bless you. I've learned some important things this evening."

Out on the street again, we ran into the mounting election fever, with processions, street orators and the mass of party posters, dominated by the red hammer and sickle, plastered on buildings, bridges, fences and windows. I thought, my two friends were going to need all the inner strength they could draw on to endure in the days ahead.

Shortly afterwards, on the train back to Jihlava, along with the legal documents I was carrying a Berlitz language course and Czech-English dictionary, ready for my lessons for the Court jurist, whose aid was so crucial for Mani. After a long evening with my parents and a late night conference with Veverka I was on my way again to Velké Meziříčí and the next moves in the battle for Mani's release.

We met once more among the archives in the bailiff's office. Again I had to come to grips with my brother's longing to vindicate himself of the charges of treachery. The issue focussed in his relationship with Karmazín. Although Mani accepted the fact of our former chauffeur's betrayal of the family and his ardent Communist convictions, Mani loved the man and felt that somehow his ideology could not prevail over a majority in the People's Court.

I did my best to convince my brother of the power of the Communist minority, not only in the Court, but its growing influence in the country. That was why, I said, I felt it was urgent to get Mani across the frontier as soon as possible. Then I described my visit to the jurist on the Court and showed him the books I had brought for the English lessons.

"You are a fox!" laughed Mani, but in the end he agreed that my strategy of winning crucial friends and avoiding confrontation was the right one.

During the remaining time I was allowed to spend with Mani that morning I drew him out about his months in this prison. For three long months he had been kept in a cell in solitary confinement, with daily threats of deportation to the uranium mines. He had no news of Alice or any of the family. Then, to his utter surprise, Mama and Papa were permitted to visit him. They had walked the ten miles from Křižanov and afterwards walked back again.

From then on life had been easier, with other visits from Mama and Papa and also from villagers and men and women whose lives he had saved. Mani had also begun to win the friendship of jailers and some workers in the county building, culminating in his work for part of each day in the Archives office. Each day, however, the threat from the People's Court hung over his head. As he recited his story he was able to give me useful information on who in Křižanov were likely to be helpful and whom I should avoid.

After a lunch with him on some of his delicacies I went to see the jurist. He took me into his small study for the English lesson. I suggested that the best means of learning a language was conversation, and he laughed when I said I had mastered six languages through the ear, without bothering the brain! I said he must repeat each of my sentences slowly and clearly.

"Our conversation today will be about revolution." This seemed to surprise him, but he repeated it lustily, adding, "You will please correct my Czech." I continued, having mapped out a topic I felt might develop our relationship.

"There is enough in the world for the need of each, but

not enough for the greed of each.'' He looked a little puzzled, but repeated the words and then nodded his head.

"If everyone is willing to share and to care, there will be enough for the needs of all.'' My pupil looked surprised and forgot to repeat. Then I really astonished him as I went on, "If we of the owning classes had taken this truth seriously, we might have avoided this bloody revolution.'' So I led him on into my philosophy that revolution means change, with the hope of improved conditions; but the change, in order to be effective, must involve not merely economic, social and political change, but also change in motives and character.

All this took a little time, but my friend emerged not only with the correct pronunciation of "change," but also some new ideas to consider. I relieved the tension every now and then by lapsing into Czech and drawing him out about his ideas.

At the end of our lesson he said, "I have much to think about.'' Then he asked, "Your brother, does he think as you do?''

I said Mani was an upright and honest man who wanted justice and peace for every man and was beginning to feel as I did about the means to achieve that goal.

My host thanked me and said he looked forward to the next lesson.

On the spur of the moment I decided to make another call on Louis and Jozy Podstadsky, arriving again at the sacred tea hour. They told me delightedly that today was the butler's day off, and they had let the rest of the servants go out and were alone.

"You probably realized last time," said Louis, "that Aloys, our butler, who was hovering around all the time, is a trusted member of the Communist Party. He listens brazenly to every word and reports it to the Party.'' That was why the family could do so little for Mani, he said sadly. Any help from them would only make matters worse for my brother.

"And for your poor parents," added Jozy, "when they were in camp here we used to see them on the street, in their rags being driven to work by those horrible creatures. Your father would be carrying bricks and your mother would be washing floors in the public buildings. They were so brave, and all we could do was look the other way."

I said of course I understood and we must do everything we could so our children would not have to grow up in this kind of world. Louis agreed vehemently and confided to me that they were seriously considering abandoning their properties and emigrating to somewhere in South America to give their children a chance. He had sounded out the authorities carefully and it had been intimated that they could leave if they gave up their estate.

I took my leave, feeling sad at the inability of this good-hearted couple to employ their generosity and concern for their friends who suffered around them.

14

Paper Chase

DAY AFTER DAY, week after week, for three months I pursued the paper chase through government offices, interview after interview, English lesson after English lesson, following every trail that might lead to the release of my parents and my brother. Then one morning in Prague I received an urgent phone call from Dr. Veverka.

His voice was guarded and low: "It is essential that Herr Mani's papers be processed immediately. I will be seeing our jurist friend today and I hope you also will call on him immediately." He said no more, but I did not need to be told that my brother's situation, precariously in the balance for some time, was now tilting dangerously.

I canceled all my plans and left for Velké Meziříčí early next morning. On greeting the jurist I spent no time on the usual pleasantries. "My brother's request to leave the country is coming before your People's Court within the next day or two."

"Yes," he said slowly, "I know." And that was all. His manner remained courteous and cool, but it was as though an invisible wall of officialdom had sprung up between us, a total bureaucratic non-communication. I felt an impotent outsider in my own country. As best I could I swallowed my sense of desolation and started on the day's lesson. As we parted on his doorstep I did my best to read into his warm handshake some message of encouragement.

I spent the night at Dr. Veverka's home and when he left for work went out and trudged the countryside, trying to work off my tension as I strode the narrow paths. In the late afternoon, back at the apartment, Veverka came rushing

148

in, his customary quiet dignity forgotten. Brandishing a fistful of papers, with their red and gold seals, he cried exultantly, "Herr Mani's exit papers!"

As I jumped up to congratulate him, he said, "But we must waste no time! He must be across the border tonight."

Together we hurried an excited and almost incredulous Mani through the formalities at the jail. Once outside, he embraced both of us in a big hug, still speechless in his gratitude. Then we packed him and his small carpet bag into the automobile and made for the train that was to bear him to the American occupation zone of Germany and his reunion with Alice in Bavaria.

It was only as we waved our last farewell to the figure, still waving as the train rounded a bend, that Veverka turned to me to say quietly, "An order arrived today from 'higher up' to include Herr Mani among those to be deported tomorrow to the Soviet Union."

Papa and Mama received the news of Mani's release with joy and said it just reaffirmed their faith in the success of my efforts. The victory prodded me to more feverish activity on my circuit of bureaucracy. I trembled at the thought of the split-second timing of Mani's release, because I had gathered from some of Veverka's veiled words that my parents' future was also precarious.

I decided to approach the local Křižanov Committee and place appeals before them also. I dreaded meeting Karmazín and was relieved that he was not in evidence. The few whom I knew on the Committee were casually friendly, although wholly non-committal. I sensed that Mani's release might have improved my parents' chances. I asked the Committee if I might be permitted to see our castle. After a slight hesitation my request was granted and a young peasant lad, dangling a great bunch of keys, was assigned to accompany me. The park, once so trim, was now thick with weeds and overgrown plants. Mama's pride and joy, the white cupids supporting the urns of roses and geraniums, had turned green with slime and the urns were empty except for some bedraggled cowslips and dandelions.

Through the great bronze doors untouched by time the stags' heads looked down on a courtyard smothered in ivy and a mass of rubble. I pictured the last time I had seen it, when Jerry and Tony, in their Tyrolean costumes, had waved a cheery farewell astride their toy horses.

Hurrying up the stairs I entered the two large drawing rooms; I thanked the Good Lord that my parents had never seen the house as it was today. Much of the furnishings had been stolen or trampled by the Russian armies. The beautiful Aubusson rug lay in shreds from nailed boots. A great rose damask sofa was in tatters from knives wielded no doubt in hatred of "bourgeois possessions." On the wall, hanging askew, was the Lazlo portrait of Mama, with me as a child leaning beside her. Pistol shots had punched out our eyes.

I moved hastily on. In the dining room I stood staring at the great silver closet, now empty, where as a child I had watched a footman spending hours shining silver and sharpening the steel knives. I wondered who now owned the seventy silver place plates.

There is perhaps nothing so desolate as beauty wantonly despoiled. "We won't go any further," I said to the boy, fumbling with his keys at the library door. Ninety-nine rooms of this desolation would kill me. He nodded unconcernedly. No doubt he held the keys to other castles and this was old stuff to him. I left the village quickly and headed for another conference with Veverka.

"I think we've made progress," he said. "Now is the time for you to accept the kind invitation promised by that Swiss friend of yours to receive your parents. Switzerland is a good neutral ground and if you can get an entrance permit from the Swiss government I think we can get them an exit permit from here."

My spirits lifted, as I felt sure of securing the Swiss entry permit. I said I would have to go there to be certain of getting it. Veverka urged my going shortly, while he pursued completion of the petitions. I was told I could obtain a visa and leave in a week's time. Before that, I went for another visit to Papa and Mama to encourage them with news of our progress.

After a few minutes Papa began stirring restlessly in his chair and clearing his throat, signs I recognized of his making up his mind about raising some issue. "Genus," he began hesitantly, "I know you are a man of strict honor and that you put your honor before material gain. Otherwise you wouldn't even be here to care for us."

I waited patiently for him to get to the point.

"When we heard that the Russians were heading our way, Mama and I collected all her jewels, put them in a jar and gave them to the one forester whom I trusted implicitly and asked him to bury the jar near his home. We ourselves buried some of our silver in the park, but of course the Russians soon found that. Now I wake at night sometimes and fear for that forester, because, as you know, Genus, all Austrian and German possessions of any kind are labeled 'Property of the State', and anyone who is caught with any 'contraband goods' is liable for the death penalty."

Papa hesitated again and then came out with, "Would you consider it honest to collect those jewels?"

I burst into laughter. "Papa, are you asking whether I consider those jewels to be state property? I most certainly do not. And what's more, they will be a heaven-sent help for your future security."

I could picture many of those jewels, the diamond coronet which glittered in Mama's dark hair when she wore it on formal occasions, the emerald bracelet that slipped up and down her arm, the great rings that Grandmother had given her, glittering on Mama's fingers, and the diamond and emerald chain Grandmother used to wear so casually around her neck. They were all that was left of the family fortune, but even so they must be worth many thousands of dollars.

Papa repeated seriously, "It's the death penalty, my son,

for absconding with the lawful property of the state.'' Then
he sat with me and drew a detailed diagram showing exactly
where the jar was buried. I left them then, taking the
diagram and promising to let them know just as soon as
I had recovered the treasure.

My immediate problem was how to get discreetly to the
forester's home fifty miles away. I would have to enlist
someone who could provide transportation without letting
him know the perilous purpose of the mission, nor involv-
ing him too deeply in the danger. I suddenly thought of
Jan, son of the director of our estate mills. He and I used
to play together as boys when I accompanied Papa on his
inspections of the mills. What was more, Jan's father used
to have an old motor bike that would be ideal for getting
to the forester's house along narrow and bumpy lanes.
Perhaps he still had it.

When I caught up with Jan I found him delighted to take
me on the back of his father's rather newer bike. All I told
him was that I had to go to the forester's house on a very
private mission. Next day at dusk we set out, with me on
the back, tightly clutching his rough jacket as we jolted our
way over country roads deeply rutted by military trucks.
We reached the end of the path which wound its way
steeply up to the house. Jan wanted to rev his engine and
make a try up the hill.

''No,'' I said very firmly, ''you'll ruin your father's
motor.''

Grudgingly he agreed and settled down to wait. I
promised I'd not be long. Soon, up above me I made out
the gleam of a candle in a window and as I came closer I
saw the forester's wife carry in the evening meal. In the
deepening dusk, using the hunting techniques the forester
had taught me many years before, I crept through the wood,
trying to avoid the crackle of twigs. Papa's diagram was clear
in my mind and I followed it until I came on a straight pine,
standing alone on a bank, its base hidden in wild strawberry
bushes.

I was kneeling down to dig at its roots, when terror gripped me as the bright beam from a flashlight behind me lit up the scene. Then the cheerful voice of Jan said, "I could hear you, Sir Doctor! I warned you that you can't walk quietly through this underbrush without heavy shoes and *Lederhosen!*"

With Jan now firmly on the scene I had to abandon my plan. Instead, I sent him looking perplexed down the hill and made a quick courtesy call on the forester and his wife, then climbed back behind Jan, who kindly took me to a place near my parents' camp.

As I walked close to the walls of their cell I whistled a line from the Scottish ballad, "I'll take the high road, and you take the low road." Sadly I whistled the "low road" notes, a signal to Papa that I had failed, but would try again.

It took another day to come up with a second plan. Franz, an old friend living in Velké Meziříčí, was willing to drive me in his big old Tatra, too big to enter the forester's lane. He asked no questions, nor did he know the forester. It seemed fool-proof.

Again, it was almost dark as I left him and climbed the path, as Franz settled back patiently to wait. This time the house was in darkness as I eased by it and came to the pine tree. I knelt, thrust my arm deep down through a bush until my fingers reached a niche in the roots. Triumphantly I grasped the jar and drew it out, dirt covered, but unbroken. I spread a handkerchief on the ground and emptied the jewels into it. Then I reburied the jar and covered the hole. I was knotting the corners of the handkerchief when I heard voices coming up the path.

Two men were talking and as they neared me, I heard one say in rough Czech, "That surely cannot be!"

The other voice answered firmly, "But it is. And we'll find them."

They're coming for the jewels, I thought, and stuffed the handkerchief into my pocket and threw myself into the bushes close by. From the thicket I saw the men enter the house; candlelight shone through a window. I was cautiously raising myself from the ground when the two men came to the door and the forester was framed in the light.

I dived to earth and lay motionless, my head buried in brambles whose thorns were scratching my face. Then, sharp pains in my neck and hands, accompanied by loud buzzing. I realized I was crouched in a swarm of bees! After what seemed an eternity, the men went inside and the door closed. I slid painfully out of the thicket and made my way to the car, bewildered and wondering whether the men had been talking about the jewels "we'll find," or something else. And the trusted forester, was he friend or betrayer? I would never know.

I was glad darkness hid the scratches and large welts rising on my face and hands. But fright and pain were forgotten later that evening as I passed Papa's camp whistling "I'll take the high road."

Back in Prague I made my preparations for the trip to Switzerland and in the course of them heard that, in addition to a search of outgoing luggage at the airport, every passenger had to submit to a personal search. All that jewelry would be hard to miss, and even harder to explain away. I planned for my departure with the greatest care. Packed and ready, bills paid, I waited in my room until I had barely time to make my plane, then rushed out to grab a cab and urged the driver to hurry to the airport.

When I arrived at the entrance I could see my plane already warming up. I strode up to the inspectors at the gate, with my overcoat hugged to my chest, thrust my ticket, passport and American-style briefcase in a lordly fashion to one inspector and impatiently pushed my suitcase at another, who ran his hands through my clothes while I tapped my foot impatiently. After a swift glance through my heavily stamped American documents the inspectors courteously waved this uncouth American through the gate.

I climbed the steps into the plane, the last passenger to board, went to my seat and laid the overcoat across its back, feeling gently with my fingers the bulge over the inside pocket, where the jewels were sewn tidily into the lining.

Several times I shuttled between Switzerland and England, savoring afresh the atmosphere in which people could come and go as they pleased. England proved to be the best market for heirloom jewelry. I stepped into a discreet small Bond Street shop and was greeted by a heavy-jowled gentleman in a frock coat. Behind a screen I spread my wares on a table where he carefully examined each piece.

"Ah!" he said, holding up Mama's coronet, "Lady X would appreciate this." He went through the collection in this fashion, matching the pieces with his clientele. Well, I thought, Dorothy won't be inheriting these beauties as the wife of the Teuber heir, as Mama had once intended, but the generous sum they provide should secure my parents' future for some time.

It took me a long three weeks to collect all the papers the meticulous Swiss required. Then I hurried back to Czechoslovakia, where I expected everything to be ready for Papa's and Mama's departure. From my hotel room in Prague I telephoned to Veverka, and all my hopes came crashing to the ground. The stubborn, violently independent People's Council had denied the petition!

A wave of hatred flooded through my heart as I visualized those stolid, smug peasant faces as they shoved aside the documents I had so laboriously compiled. The truth lay before them, but they had dismissed it with their crass arrogance. Veverka's voice was shaking as he hung up. I buried my face in my hands and gave way to bitterness and a great longing for vengeance. Then came despair, as I tried to blot out from my mind the picture of my parents' faces as I broke the news.

Finally I slipped to my knees, uttering an incoherent prayer of helplessness. Amidst the torrent of bewilderment one annoying and irrelevant thought kept repeating itself – the name of Franzie Schonborn. Franzie was a Prince, a lively, witty and debonair rogue with whom I had explored the night life of Prague in my youth. I hadn't seen this man for twenty years. Every time I brushed away his name, it returned. Irritated, I rose from my knees.

At lunch, on a sudden impulse, I asked my waiter whether Herr Schonborn – I carefully avoided the title "Prince" – was around these days in Prague.

"But certainly, sir, you will probably find him in the bar."

And there he was, the same old Franzie apart from the wear and tear of twenty years, leaning casually on the bar, but resplendent now in full regalia of the Czech Army, bedecked with ribbons and medals. Although he had consorted almost exclusively with our Austrian families, we knew him as one who cherished his ancient Czech origins. As I stared at him now I thought that his ostentatious identification with his ancestry smacked more than a little of self-protection.

Franzie greeted me joyfully and we chatted gaily of earlier days. Then, with no change of expression, he asked , "Got troubles?" I nodded.

"Parents?" I nodded again.

"Tomorrow at ten o'clock in our cafe," he murmured and drifted off to chat at a nearby table.

There was no doubt about which cafe; it was a quiet, small restaurant that had been our favorite haunt. When I arrived promptly, Franzie was sitting at a corner table, still in his uniform, but without the medals and ribbons. His manner was totally changed as he tersely unfolded his story of the use of his record and position in the Czech Army, regarded with respect by government and civilians alike, to aid his fellow aristocrats to escape across the border.

I burst out, "You are the Czech Scarlet Pimpernel!" He and I had enjoyed together the tales of Baroness Orczy's fictional hero who had rescued aristocrats from the guillotine in the French Revolution.

He brushed my exclamation aside. "Tell me how things stand with your parents."

I related the details of their imprisonment, of all my

tedious chase of the documents needed for their release, and of their recent failure. As he listened intently he broke in with occasional comments – "You won him over?" "How much did that document cost you?"

He just nodded at the recital of my final defeat, as though it were an old story to him. He stared out at the passers-by on the street and I waited. Finally, he asked, "Both your mother and father were born in Austria, right?" I nodded.

Franzie gave a great grin. "Then we have it!" For the next ten minutes he took me through the details of a clever ruse whereby Papa and Mama could be exempted from the regulations under which the People's Court had rejected the exit documents. With a little manipulation of the law, my parents' foreign birth could give them the right to leave the country.

I did not really follow my friend's intricate maneuvers, but in the face of my lingering doubts, Franzie said forcibly, "It will work. These new People's Courts are dreadfully afraid of losing face should they make mistakes in any legal decisions."

Franzie rose and put his hand on my shoulder. "Grüss Gott, Genus!" And he sauntered out of the restaurant.

Lawyer Veverka took new heart. Under his meticulous guidance I once more set the legal wheels in motion, churning out sworn statement after statement. We stayed away from Mama and Papa while this was going on, until the day when I had the precious papers for their release. As I crossed the courtyard of the camp towards their cell I glimpsed Papa's face looking out through the barred window. How many times, I wondered, had he watched and waited?

An hour later, still dazed with joy, Mama and Papa walked out of their cell and through the gate with Veverka and me. No more arm bands, all four of us walked together – in dignity on the sidewalk. A few hours later, Papa and Mama began their new life in Switzerland.

Epilogue
by Jerry von Teuber

My FATHER'S active life did not end with his arrival with his parents in Switzerland. He took them from Geneva to South Tyrol, where my grandmother Anna von Teuber's family owned a small but historic chateau. South Tyrol, another area lost to Austria as the result of World War I, was ceded to Italy in 1919, stranding over 200,000 German-speaking people in the new Italy.

Immediately realizing the possibilities for impacting one of the longest-standing minority conflicts in Europe, my father invited Frank Buchman and some of his friends to spend the winter of 1947 with the von Teubers in their castle. My mother, my brothers Tony and John and I were there as well. What followed was the beginning of a process that cleared the way for what the *Washington Post* later called "the resolution of one of Central Europe's longest disputes about the rights of minorities."

His experiences in Czechoslovakia and subsequently in South Tyrol confirmed my father, and my mother with him, in a life-long quest for individual and national reconciliation, often in partnership with his Moral Re-Armament associates. The lessons he learned in answering bitterness through a change in attitude were to be repeated in innumerable encounters throughout Europe and Latin America in the years that followed. He died in San Francisco in March, 1965, at the age of 63.

This is not the time or place to tell that story. That will be another book. My brothers and I only wish that he and Mother had lived to see the release of his country from the grip of the Soviet Union and the renewal of bonds with the

West. There is no doubt in our minds that he would have been deeply exercised over the issues now dividing his homeland and would have been actively involved in trying to bring a solution based on a meeting of minds. He would surely have rejoiced, however, that the split between Czechs and Slovaks was accomplished without the violence that is tearing Yugoslavia apart today.

In early 1991, a few months after the "velvet revolution" broke the Communist control of Czechoslovakia, my brothers and I, who now live in the United States, made a brief visit to the country. Conditions were still chaotic, but we were able to drive to the district where Grandfather had presided over his large estates. We were overwhelmed by all the evidence of neglect and breakdown in the countryside – farms and whole villages in need of basic repair and crops gone to waste in the fields because of the disappearance of markets after the severing of economic ties with Russia. We were able to drive to the village of Křižanov where Grosspapa's castle stood. Here, too, was a desolate scene, with dreary, pock-marked cottages and the air of a depressed community. The castle itself stood in sharp contrast, its outer walls beautifully restored and gleaming with their original glint of yellow; it had been taken over by the state as a care center for 150 mentally retarded, with a staff of 70 to look after them. Our visit to Křižanov was brief and we had little opportunity to meet people or learn about their life.

Five months later, however, I was able to return, together with my wife Barbara, after my uncle Mani, Father's brother, living a few miles away in Germany, had made contact with the community of Křižanov and prepared the villagers for our coming. We first paid a visit to the castle while the residents were being given their evening meal and put to bed.

As we were shown around the building I explained to Barbara that only the original huge drawing-room bore any resemblance to the photographs of the rooms which my parents had treasured and passed on to me. It was now being used as the recreation-music room for the institution. The other great rooms had been partitioned into small ones. The massive furniture and beautiful furnishings had all disappeared. I learned, too, that the long wing, which Grandfather had added to the castle to house offices for the managers of the 11,000 acres of the agricultural properties, was now used as apartments for village families.

We were treated with the greatest politeness by the staff, but this dimmed in comparison with the welcome we received when we were led to the home of the Mayor of the village and her husband, head of the regional hospital. They ushered us into their home and seated us before a seven-course banquet featuring wonderful Czech national dishes made with vegetables grown in their newly acquired greenhouse, around which they later escorted us. After the meal they begged us to stay in a fine guest home, which they said would be available for us whenever we could visit Křižanov. Then they went on to shower us with gifts, precious possessions they had treasured over the years. When we in turn presented them with our gift, a golden miniature we had brought for them from Spain, the Mayor clasped it to her bosom and wept.

The couple took us on a walking-tour of the village, a highlight of which was a visit to the first privately owned business in town, a pastry and ice-cream shop, charmingly decorated in marble and wood. Here a further surprise awaited us: the owner stepped forward, immaculate in glistening starched chef's hat and uniform and bearing a tray of aged Czech vermouth and marinated orange slices. Bowing deeply to me he proffered a toast, "Herr Baron, welcome to our Křižanov!" Then, turning to Barbara, "And to you, dear Lady!" He went on, "My father was the Master Baker at the castle when I was a child and my mother was one of the cooks. I recall the day the word was spread through the town, 'The Americans are here,' and then we saw you and your little brother taking walks with your nurse. Never did I dream that one day I would see you again and that you would step into my shop. I am deeply honored . . .'' And he broke into tears, and so did Barbara and I. Thereupon he produced a veritable feast of Czech pastries and desserts specially prepared for us – five dessert courses in all! And this just on top of a seven-course dinner!

As we talked over his early recollections of Tony and me villagers streamed past, viewing us from a respectful distance, then accompanied us to the village church, a lovely well-kept structure dating back to the year 1200. We attended Mass at which to our surprise at five o'clock on a weekday afternoon, many village faithful were present, including many young men. The service concluded with all the verses of ''Nearer, my God, to Thee'' sung in Czech, with Barbara and me singing in English. The service ended and we stood with overflowing hearts as villagers, with no common language between us, hugged Barbara and gripped my hand.

As the church emptied I asked the aged pastor's assistant if he would unlock the family chapel, next to the castle, so that we could have a few quiet moments there. The pastor had held the only key and guarded it very carefully. We entered the chapel, an austere building close to a thousand years old and reminding me of an old Quaker meetinghouse. Around it stood 250-year-old trees and as the heavy wooden doors swung open we were bathed in the glowing golden light streaming through their leaves into the windows. The baroque chapel had been designed by the Italian architect Santini. When the invading Russians had pillaged our castle they had stolen all the artwork and gold leaf from the chapel, but these had been painstakingly restored at the intitiative of the old priest, aided especially by generous Swiss.

Set into the floor in front of the altar lies an old burial crypt marked by a heavy iron ring. Etched in its center, worn thin by many feet, is a faintly discernible crest. I held my signet-ring close to the crest so that the people around us could see that they were identical. It was a special moment.

In that quiet place, surrounded by men and women who had lived through tyranny, deprivation and hardships such as I had never experienced, I found my mind going back to Father. I felt his presence. Here was a man who had shown care and kindness, hope and understanding, beyond the circle of his family and friends. Surely I had seen today how those seeds had blossomed despite sharp differences of class, race and nationality. Here was a quiet testimony to the hope and humanity one man could bequeath to his fellows.

Finally, I would like to conclude with an expression of appreciation and gratitude to Dad's long-time friend, Basil Entwistle, whose collaboration in the preparation of this manuscript has resulted in a book of which both my parents would have been proud.

Tucson, Arizona
May, 1993